T0355072

Cambridge Lower Secondary **Complete English**

Series Editor: Dean Roberts
Alan Jenkins, Mark Pedroz, Jane Arredondo, Annabel Charles, Tony Parkinson

Jedidah Kithia, Sujata Paul Maliah, Khalid Qenaway

Second Edition

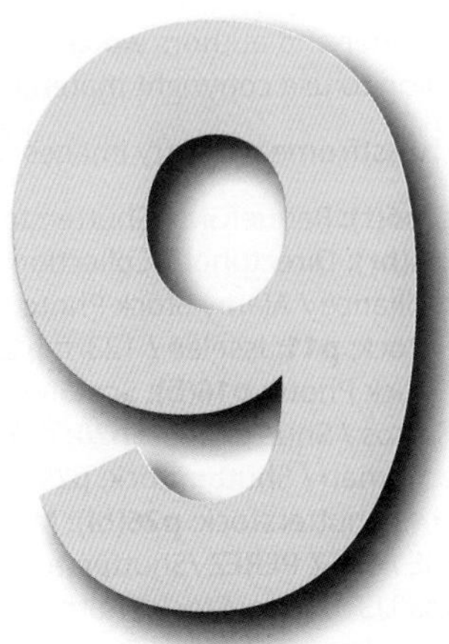

OXFORD
UNIVERSITY PRESS

OXFORD
UNIVERSITY PRESS

Great Clarendon Street, Oxford, OX2 6DP, United Kingdom

Oxford University Press is a department of the University of Oxford.

It furthers the University's objective of excellence in research, scholarship, and education by publishing worldwide. Oxford is a registered trade mark of Oxford University Press in the UK and in certain other countries

© Oxford University Press 2022

The moral rights of the authors have been asserted

First published in 2022

All rights reserved. No part of this publication may be reproduced, stored in a retrieval system, or transmitted, in any form or by any means, without the prior permission in writing of Oxford University Press, or as expressly permitted by law, by licence or under terms agreed with the appropriate reprographics rights organization. Enquiries concerning reproduction outside the scope of the above should be sent to the Rights Department, Oxford University Press, at the address above.

You must not circulate this work in any other form and you must impose this same condition on any acquirer

British Library Cataloguing in Publication Data

Data available

978-1-38-201939-2

978-1-38-201945-3 (ebook)

10 9 8 7 6 5 4

Paper used in the production of this book is a natural, recyclable product made from wood grown in sustainable forests.

The manufacturing process conforms to the environmental regulations of the country of origin.

Printed in China by Shanghai Offset Printing Products Ltd

Acknowledgements

The publisher and authors would like to thank the following for permission to use copyright material:

Cover: beastfromeast/Getty Images

Photos: **p6(t):** RaquelGM / Shutterstock; **p6(bl):** vadymvdrobot / 123rf; **p6(br):** Directphoto Collection / Alamy Stock Photo; **p7:** dpa picture alliance / Alamy Stock Photo; **p8:** Ming-Hsiang Chuang / Shutterstock; **p11:** Isselee / 123rf; **p16(t):** Everett Collection Inc / Alamy Stock Photo; **p16(b):** ScotStock / Alamy Stock Photo; **p19:** ArtOfPhotos / Shutterstock; **p20:** dragonimages / 123rf; **p21:** Venera Salman / Shutterstock; **p25:** suhovhd / Shutterstock; **p26(t):** Merlin74 / Shutterstock; **p26(bl):** Microgen / Shutterstock; **p26(br):** ENRIQUE ALAEZ PEREZ /Shutterstock; **p27:** krugloff / Shutterstock; **p28:** Sipa US / Alamy Stock Photo; **p30:** schusterbauer.com / Shutterstock; **p36:** Buckley, R., Morris, M., Appleby, J., King, T., O'Sullivan, D., & Foxhall, L. (2013). 'The king in the car park': New light on the death and burial of Richard III in the Grey Friars church, Leicester, in 1485. Antiquity, 87(336), 519-538. doi:10.1017/S0003598X00049103; **p37:** Stocktrek Images, Inc. / Alamy Stock Photo; **p38:** wawritto / 123rf; **p39:** wavebreakmedia / Shutterstock; **p41:** GAS-photo / Shutterstock; **p43:** elnavegante / Shutterstock; **p44:** UPI / Alamy Stock Photo; **p46(t):** Fredrick Kippe / Alamy Stock Photo; **p46(bl):** sbonsi / Shutterstock; **p46(br):** Mickael Chavet / Project Daybreak / Alamy Stock Photo; **p47(l):** lev radin / Shutterstock; **p47(c):** jeremy sutton-hibbert / Alamy Stock Photo; **p47(r):** ZUMA Press / Alamy Stock Photo; **p48:** AA Film Archive / Alamy Stock Photo; **p49:** 7106108800 / 123rf; **p52:** PA Images / Alamy Stock Photo; **p57:** True Touch Lifestyle / Shutterstock; **p59:** Fer Gregory / Shutterstock; **p60:** Chronicle / Alamy Stock Photo; **p64:** happiness time / Shutterstock; **p66(t):** Vertyr/Shutterstock; **p66(bl):** potowizard / Shutterstock; **p66(br):** Production Perig / Shutterstock; **p67:** Hananeko_Studio / Shutterstock; **p68:** Nido Huebl / Shutterstock; **p69:** Watch The World / Shutterstock; **p72:** Michael Liggett / Shutterstock; **p75:** jhorrocks / Getty Images; **p78:** Hemis / Alamy Stock Photo; **p80:** Phant / Shutterstock; **p81:** Sergey Borisov / Alamy Stock Photo; **p84:** Volodymyr Goinyk / Alamy Stock Photo; **p86(t):** Dmitry Rukhlenko / Shutterstock; **p86(bl):** Castleski / Alamy Stock Photo; **p86(br):** StoryTime Studio /Shutterstock; **p90:** Fotos593 / Shutterstock; **p92:** Sinesp / Shutterstock; **p94:** Volodymyr Burdiak / Shutterstock; **p98:** Cavan Images / Alamy Stock Photo; **p99:** smontgom65 / 123rf; **p100:** This Is Me / Shutterstock; **p101:** sergign / 123rf; **p102:** ploypemuk / Shutterstock; **p103:** Soloviova Liudmyla / Shutterstock; **p104(t):** Vadim Sadovski / Shutterstock; **p104(bl):** DC Studio / Shutterstock; **p104(br):** Gorodenkoff / Shutterstock; **p105:** studiovin / Shutterstock; **p106:** kesu87 / 123rf; **p107:** Perfect Wave / Shutterstock; **p109:** ensup / 123rf; **p110:** Sergey Nivens / Shutterstock; **p112:** retrorocket / Shutterstock; **p113:** Ola-ola / Shutterstock; **p114:** Reuters / Alamy Stock Photo; **p115:** DC Stock / Alamy Stock Photo; **p122:** SeventyFour / Shutterstock; **p123:** Antonio Guillem / Shutterstock; **p124(t):** DNZ Creative Design / Shutterstock; **p124(bl):** D and D Photo Sudbury / Shutterstock; **P124(br):** Helen E. Grose / Shutterstock; **p125:** Scott E Read / Shutterstock; **p127:** Ging o_o / Shutterstock; **p130:** Art Collection 2 / Alamy Stock Photo; **p131:** Chantal de Bruijne / SHutterstock; **p132:** IanDagnall Computing / Alamy Stock Photo; **p134:** Willyam Bradberry / Shutterstock; **p138:** Nneirda / Shutterstock; **p142:** mwilliamsnz / 123rf; **p144(t):** Dmitry Rukhlenko / Shutterstock; 144(bl): Tukaram.Karve / Shutterstock; 144(br): Andrzej Kubik / Shutterstock; **p146:** Earl D. Walker / Shutterstock; **p148:** SCOTTCHAN / Shutterstock; **p150:** SIHASAKPRACHUM / Shutterstock; **p151:** Lucy.Brown / Shutterstock; **p159:** Mike Richter / Shutterstock; **p160:** Andrzej Wilusz / Shutterstock; **p161:** NORTH DEVON PHOTOGRAPHY / Shutterstock; **p164(t):** pio3 / Shutterstock; **p164(bl):** Kyrylo Glivin / Shutterstock; **p164(br):** Paapaya / Shutterstock; **p165:** Anadolu Agency / Getty Images; **p170:** Migel / Shutterstock; **p173:** Sergey Nivens / Shutterstock; **p174:** Tetra Images, LLC / Alamy Stock Photo; **p176:** Antonio Guillem / Shutterstock; **p178:** colinspics / Alamy Stock Photo; **p181:** REUTERS / Alamy Stock Photo; **p182:** Alex_Traksel / Shutterstock; **p184:** ocskaymark / 123rf.

Artwork by Integra Software, Q2A Media, Six Red Marbles and Oxford University Press.

Every effort has been made to contact copyright holders of material reproduced in this book. Any omissions will be rectified in subsequent printings if notice is given to the publisher.

This Student Book refers to the Cambridge Lower Secondary English (0861) Syllabus published by Cambridge Assessment International Education.

This work has been developed independently from and is not endorsed by or otherwise connected with Cambridge Assessment International Education.

Contents

In every unit there are listening tasks. Your teacher may play the audio for you, or you can listen to the audio on the website using the QR code.

Website: www.oxfordsecondary.com/9781382019392

Introduction to Student Book 9

Welcome to Oxford's **Cambridge Lower Secondary Complete English Student Book 9**. This book and the student workbook will support you and your teacher as you engage with Stage 9 of the Cambridge curriculum framework.

It aims to encourage you in becoming:

- **Confident** in your English skills and your ability to express yourself
- **Responsible** for your own learning and responsive to and respectful of others
- **Reflective** as a learner so that you can be a life-long learner – not just in school now
- **Innovative** and ready for new challenges as a global citizen
- **Engaged** in both academic and social situations.

Student Book and Workbook

There are some great features in your Stage 9 book. Here's an explanation of how they work.

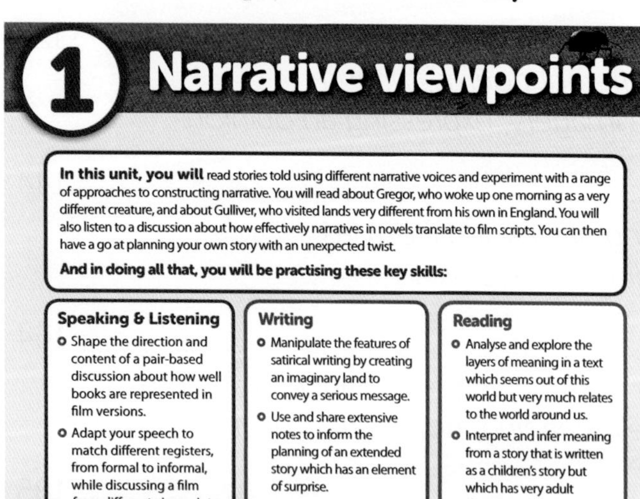

1 Narrative viewpoints

In this unit, you will read stories told using different narrative voices and experiment with a range of approaches to constructing narrative. You will read about Gregor, who woke up one morning as a very different creature, and about Gulliver, who visited lands very different from his own in England. You will also listen to a discussion about how effectively narratives in novels translate to film scripts. You can then have a go at planning your own story with an unexpected twist.

And in doing all that, you will be practising these key skills:

Speaking & Listening
- Shape the direction and content of a pair-based discussion about how well books are represented in film versions.
- Adapt your speech to match different registers, from formal to informal, while discussing a film from different viewpoints.

Writing
- Manipulate the features of satirical writing by creating an imaginary land to convey a serious message.
- Use and share extensive notes to inform the planning of an extended story which has an element of surprise.

Reading
- Analyse and explore the layers of meaning in a text which seems out of this world but very much relates to the world around us.
- Interpret and infer meaning from a story that is written as a children's story but which has very adult themes.

At the start of every unit, you'll see the type of page above. It gives you a quick summary of what the unit will be about and the main skills you will be learning and practising.

The units look at the past, the present world we live in and the possibilities of the future. The work in the units encourages you to practise the curriculum skills you need for success by exploring relevant and contemporary topics such as science, communities, influencers, tourism and investigation. There are also units that focus on narratives, drama and the work of the poet William Blake.

Through the Thinking time and Speaking & Listening features, you will get the chance to express what you already know about a theme or topic, think critically and find out more from your classmates whilst exploring new ideas.

Reading

You will read about a character in literature called Gregor, who was no longer human when he woke one morning! This extract will help you learn how narrative works and, in particular, how a writer controls narrative. You will also read about a drought in Trinidad and how it affected the local people. Here, you will learn about how writers choose descriptive words with care. A different kind of reading will also introduce you to a real-life explorer who walked the entire length of the Amazon river. And you will also read about King Richard III of England as well as poems about sharks, snakes and tigers!

Use the Word clouds to learn new vocabulary, exploring meanings and usage in context. The Glossary features will help you with words or phrases that you may not find in a dictionary because they are uncommon, colloquial or technical.

Listening

You will listen to a talk about the early life of Nelson Mandela, a discussion where four

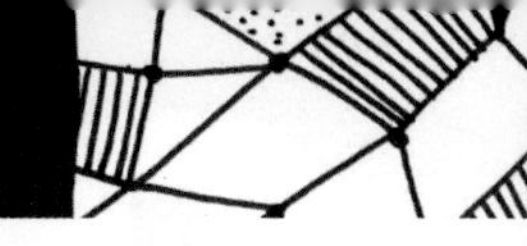

students talk about their very different cultural backgrounds, a lively discussion where two people debate if the book is always better than the film and a radio broadcast about the discovery of the bones of an English king who died hundreds of years ago. When you listen to all of these people, and more, you will be practising your skills of listening to locate details, listening to understand the gist of what is being said and listening to make inferences – trying to work out what people really mean!

Writing workshops

Most of the units have a workshop in which you will focus either on creative writing – stories, a drama script and your own poetry – or on writing non-fiction pieces.

You will practise using a wide range of writing styles for different purposes: a persuasive essay, arguing whether you should be allowed to listen to music while you study at school, a review of some new poems, a travel blog, a TV screenplay about a detective trying to solve a crime, a story based on a character you have created, and a summary of an article on how best to get a good night's sleep!

Speaking

Learning through talking is really important. You will take part in a wide range of speaking contexts – talking by yourself, working with a partner or taking part in small group discussions. Learning how and when to make your contributions is a key skill for success in tests and exams, but also in life. The speaking tasks include a group poetry game, reading some poems out loud by yourself, discussing which roles each member of your group will play on an expedition to walk along the Amazon river, working out with a partner what it is about influential people that helps them become powerful, being in the hot seat as a famous person, giving a multi-media presentation about the place where you live, and playing your part in a range of dramatic pieces.

Language development

There are also activities to improve your language awareness and help you develop your use of language, including your grammar, spelling and punctuation. In this Stage 9 book, there is a focus on using topic sentences to good effect, abstract nouns, transition and connecting words, using discourse markers in speech, choosing adjectives carefully, getting to grips with complex sentences by experimenting with punctuation, making sure you use a wider range of sentence types in your writing and exploring words that end in *-tic*.

Vocabulary

Learning new words and, perhaps more importantly, learning exactly how they should be used is a key element of this series of books. There are lots of word building exercises for you to extend and enhance your vocabulary. Don't expect to know all the words you encounter – this book will help you build up your vocabulary.

Assessment workshops

As you move towards the formal assessment of tests and exams (and perhaps preparing for the IGCSE English course), the Assessment workshop in each unit will help you practise the skills you need. Each workshop invites you to self-assess and reflect on your own learning by presenting you with tasks and questions like the ones you will find in the Cambridge Lower Secondary Checkpoint test. There are also sample student responses which you can explore and even mark. In addition, there are many useful tips to help you improve key skills.

1 Narrative viewpoints

In this unit, you will read stories told using different narrative voices and experiment with a range of approaches to constructing narrative. You will read about Gregor, who woke up one morning as a very different creature, and about Gulliver, who visited lands very different from his own in England. You will also listen to a discussion about how effectively narratives in novels translate to film scripts. You can then have a go at planning your own story with an unexpected twist.

And in doing all that, you will be practising these key skills:

Speaking & Listening

- Shape the direction and content of a pair-based discussion about how well books are represented in film versions.
- Adapt your speech to match different registers, from formal to informal, while discussing a film from different viewpoints.

Writing

- Manipulate the features of satirical writing by creating an imaginary land to convey a serious message.
- Use and share extensive notes to inform the planning of an extended story which has an element of surprise.

Reading

- Analyse and explore the layers of meaning in a text which seems out of this world but very much relates to the world around us.
- Interpret and infer meaning from a story that is written as a children's story but which has very adult themes.

Assessment workshop

You will gain practice in the key assessment skill of writing an extended story using a controlled and fluent narrative voice as well as your creativity.

Thinking time

1. In what ways does reading exercise the mind?
2. Do we need illustrations in books to see what the characters look like? Why/why not?
3. Look at the last quotation on the right. How can a book 'bite' or 'sting' you?

"Reading is to the mind what exercise is to the body."
Joseph Addison

"'... and what is the use of a book,' thought Alice, 'without pictures or conversation?'"
Lewis Carroll

"I think you should only read those books which bite and sting you."
Franz Kafka

Types of novels – fiction genres

Here is a list of popular fiction genres:

children's	fantasy	science-fiction
murder mystery	adventure	westerns
young adult	romance	
thriller	historical	

Answer these questions, explaining your views.

1. Which genre(s) do you prefer? Explain why.
2. Which sort of novel(s) would you never choose in a library or book shop? Why?

Speaking & Listening – comparing the film and the book

Talk about a film you have seen which is based on a book you know. Answer these questions.

1. Were the characters in the film better than the characters in the book?
2. What makes a movie character memorable?
3. Can you think of a character in a book who reminds you of a real person? Explain your answer.
4. Why may characters in films sometimes be confused with the actors who play them?
5. Think about how young people of your age may have lived during the past, before cinema and TV were invented. Discuss:
   - **a** what they did for entertainment
   - **b** what books they may have read and why.
6. Do you think reading for entertainment will be something future generations will do? Explain your answer.

Metamorphosis

As Gregor Samsa woke one morning from uneasy dreams, he found himself transformed into some kind of monstrous **vermin**. He lay on his hard, armour-like back, and if he lifted his head a little, he could see his curved brown **abdomen**, divided by arch-shaped ridges, and domed so high that the **bedspread**, on the brink of slipping off, could hardly stay put. His many legs, **miserably** thin in comparison with his size otherwise, flickered helplessly before his eyes.

'What has happened to me?' he thought. It was not a dream. His room, a proper human being's room, rather too small, lay peacefully between its four familiar walls. (…)

Gregor's gaze then turned towards the window, and the **murky** weather – one could hear the raindrops striking the **window-sill** – made him quite **melancholy**. 'What if I went on sleeping for a while and forgot all these **idiocies**?', he thought, but that was quite impossible, as he was used to sleeping on his right side and in his present state he was unable to get himself into this position. However energetically he flung himself onto his right side, whenever he did so he would rock onto his back again. He must have tried a hundred times, shutting his eyes so that he didn't have to see his **jittery** legs, and he only gave over when he began to feel a slight ache in his side, something he had never felt before. (…)

He felt a slight itching high on his abdomen. He pushed himself slowly on his back towards the bedpost so that he could lift his head more easily; he found the itching spot, which was covered with lots of little white dots he had no idea how to interpret. He tried to probe the spot with one of his legs, but drew back at once, for the moment he touched it he was swept by cold shivers. (…)

Throwing off the bedspread was quite simple; he needed only to puff himself up a little and it fell down of its own accord. But after that it got difficult, particularly because he was so uncommonly wide. He would have needed arms and hands to raise himself; but instead of those, he had only these many little legs, which were continually fluttering about, and which he could not control anyhow. If he tried to bend one of them, it was

abdomen	**melancholy**
bedspread	**miserably**
idiocy	**murky**
jittery	**vermin**
mass	**window-sill**

Glossary

at any price under any circumstances

had no idea how to interpret was not sure about or did not know what to think

swept by cold shivers to start trembling

uncommonly wide being of great or more than average width the first to stretch; and if he finally managed to get this leg to do what he wanted, all the others were flapping about meanwhile in the most intense and painful excitement, as if they had been let loose. (...)

So he attempted to get his upper body out of the bed first, cautiously turning his head towards the edge. This worked easily enough, and in the end, despite its width and weight, the **mass** of his body slowly followed the way his head was turning. But when at last he held his head in the air outside the bed, he became afraid of moving any further forward in this way, for if he did finally let himself drop, it would need a sheer miracle for his head to remain unharmed. And right now was no time to lose consciousness, not at any price; he would sooner stay in bed.

From *Metamorphosis* by Franz Kafka

Understanding

Answer the following questions.

1. Why can't Gregor get out of bed?
   Write one sentence in your own words. Give a quotation from the passage to support your answer.
2. Suggest what type of 'vermin' Gregor has turned into.
3. In the last paragraph, Gregor becomes afraid. What is he afraid of, and why?
4. Explain in your own words what Gregor might be thinking in the final sentence: 'And right now was no time to lose consciousness, not at any price; he would sooner stay in bed.'
5. From whose point of view does the author tell the story? Give a reason to support your answer.
6. Can you think of a time when you just didn't feel yourself? A time when you felt odd, or different, as if you didn't quite recognise the world around you. Convey the experience to a classmate.

Narrative viewpoint

This extract from *Metamorphosis* is written in the third person, using Gregor's name and *he*. The author, Franz Kafka, uses an omniscient narrator who knows everything that is happening, but he is writing from Gregor's point of view.

If you are writing someone's thoughts, you can put them in quotation marks. Quotation marks around a character's thoughts go into the main body of a paragraph. Quotation marks in a dialogue should start a new line, indenting the first word for each new person speaking.

Developing your language – writing a story from the main character's point of view

1. The only person in this extract is Gregor. Find a sentence in quotation marks. Why does the author use quotation marks if Gregor is not talking to anyone?
2. The author describes Gregor's room and the weather. Why do you think the author includes this information?
3. Gregor 'found himself transformed into some kind of monstrous vermin'. Find another way to say the opening sentence to grab your reader's attention. Do not use an exclamation mark.

Word builder

1. The author describes Gregor's new size and shape, with an 'armour-like back'. Make a list of words and phrases the author uses to describe Gregor's beetle body.
2. Make a list of words and phrases that describe the movement of Gregor's 'jittery' legs. Do these words suggest that Gregor has much control over his legs' movements?
3. The title of Kafka's story is *Metamorphosis*. Use a dictionary and explain in your own words why Kafka may have chosen this title.

Using semi-colons in complex sentences

The semi-colon (;) allows a writer to join two or more sentences on the same subject into one sentence. It is used to:

- link phrases that are about the same thing or that complement each other in some way.
  Example:
  'Throwing off the bedspread was quite simple; he needed only to puff himself up a little and it fell down of its own accord.'
- join two or more ideas that are of equal importance.
  Example:
  'He would have needed arms and hands to raise himself; but instead of those, he had only these many little legs, which were continually fluttering about, and which he could not control anyhow.'
- separate items in a description or a list.
  Example:
  'He pushed himself slowly on his back towards the bedpost so that he could lift his head more easily; he found the itching spot, which was covered with lots of little white dots he had no idea how to interpret.'

Remember

A complex sentence has one main clause and one or more subordinate or dependent clauses. The main clause is the most important part of the sentence.

Answer the following questions.

1. Look at the following sentence:

   'Throwing off the bedspread was quite simple; he needed only to puff himself up a little and it fell down of its own accord.'

   What does the second part of the sentence, after the semi-colon, explain about the first half?

2. Look at paragraph 4 in the *Metamorphosis* extract.

   a How many sentences are there?

   b Rewrite the paragraph using only simple and compound sentences.

   c Why did the author choose to use a semi-colon in a long complex sentence rather than shorter sentences?

Lilliput

Before the events in this extract, Gulliver was shipwrecked and had to swim for his life. He reached shore in the country of Lilliput, where he was made a prisoner and carried inland.

I lay down on the grass, which was very short and soft, where I slept sounder than ever I remember to have done in my life, and as I reckoned, above nine hours; for when I awaked, it was just daylight. I attempted to rise, but was not able to stir: for as I happened to lie on my back, I found my arms and legs were strongly fastened on each side to the ground; and my hair, which was long and thick, tied down in the same manner. I likewise felt several slender **ligatures** across my body, from my armpits to my thighs. I could only look upwards; the sun began to grow hot, and the light offended mine eyes. I heard a confused noise about me, but in the **posture** I lay, could see nothing except the sky.

In a little time, I felt something alive moving on my left leg, which advancing gently forward over my breast, came almost up to my chin; when bending mine eyes downwards as much as I could, I **perceived** it to be a human creature not six inches high, with a bow and arrow in his hands, and a **quiver** at his back. In the meantime, I felt at least forty more of the same kind (as I **conjectured**) following the first. I was in the utmost astonishment, and roared so loud, that they all ran back in a fright; and some of them, as I was afterward told, were hurt with the falls they got by leaping from my sides upon the ground. However, they soon returned, and one of them, who ventured so far as to get a full sight of my face, lifting up his hands and eyes by way of admiration, cried out in a **shrill**, but distinct voice, *Hekinah degul*: the others repeated the same words several times, but I then knew not what they meant. I lay all this while, as the reader may believe, in great uneasiness.

From *Gulliver's Travels* by Jonathan Swift

Remember

In a first person narrative, the viewpoint is told using *I, us, our, ourselves*, and is directed at the reader. A famous example is in Charlotte Bronte's novel, *Jane Eyre*: 'Reader: I married him.'

Word cloud

conjectured	**posture**
ligatures	**quiver**
perceived	**shrill**

Glossary

likewise similarly

offended to cause unpleasant feeling

to stir to move

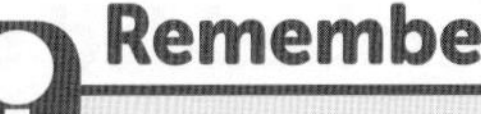

Understanding

1. Gulliver swims ashore and finds a pleasant place to lie down and sleep. Why?
2. Why can't Gulliver move when he wakes up? Find a quotation in the extract to support your answer.
3. How does the author show the reader that the people of Lilliput are very small? Find words or phrases in the extract to support your answer.
4. Gulliver hears words in the language of Lilliput. Suggest a possible meaning for '*Hekinah degul*'. Use the context of the phrase to help you.
5. Look at how many times the author uses the first person *I* in the opening paragraph. The author writes about what happens to Gulliver as if he is a real person telling his story. But this is a fictional first person. Why do you think Jonathan Swift chose to write in the first person as if he is Gulliver?
6. Gulliver travels to three more very different places in the novel: a land where he is minuscule among giants, a land of scientists and a flying island of philosophers. If he were to have visited a fifth place, what type of being might inhabit it?

Remember

Archaic language is no longer in everyday use. It is old-fashioned. You can use the context in which it is written to work out what it means.

Global Perspectives

Jonathan Swift uses the story of Gulliver as a satire to make a political comment about the belief system of his own country of Britain and how it should be reformed to be more caring of poorer people. Satire is a method used by writers to make us think about what should change for the better. Analyse a satire you know about from your own culture. How much do you agree with it?

Word builder

Look at the words and phrases in the Word cloud. Try to work out the meaning of each word, using the context in the extract.

Now have some fun and use each word in a modern and informal context.

Example:

"Hey, I was thinking that we could go to that gig tonight. Only it's 2021 and I conjecture that we'll probably need vaccine passports to get in."

Using embedded clauses

Embedded clauses are called subordinate or dependent clauses because they are part of a larger sentence but they are not the most important piece of information.

Example:

Fatima lost her bag.
Fatima's mother gave her the bag for her birthday.
Fatima lost it (the bag) on her way home.

We can join these sentences together using an embedded clause and an adverbial.

Fatima lost her bag, which her mother had given her on her birthday (embedded clause), on her way home (adverbial phrase).

Remember

A clause is part of a sentence which requires more information to create a full and proper sentence.

Answer the following questions.

1. Here are the beginnings, middles and ends of four mixed-up sentences with embedded clauses. Sort these and join the parts together to make longer sentences.

   You need to add a *who* or *which* to each sentence. You also need to put in the correct punctuation. **Example:**

   My uncle, who is very old-fashioned, doesn't have a TV.

the elephants	have convincing characters	looked too human to me
my uncle	had been walking for hundreds of miles	keep me reading all night
the Hobbits in the movie	(who) is very old-fashioned	finally found water
the best sort of books	according to the author have furry feet	doesn't have a TV

2. Write three sentences of your own with embedded clauses. Start your embedded clause with a *which* or *who* connective. Don't forget to use commas.

Adverbial phrases

Answer these questions.

1. What do the following adverbial phrases have in common?
   - As Gregor Samsa woke one morning from uneasy dreams . . .
   - In a little time, I felt something alive moving on my leg . . .
   - In the meantime, I felt at least forty more . . .
2. Write two short sentences with an adverbial that show *where* something is happening. Don't forget to put the comma after the adverbial phrase. **Example:**

   Lying back in bed, he decided not to get up.
3. Write two short sentences with an adverbial that show *how* something is happening. **Example:**

   Moving cautiously, hoping no one would hear him, he opened the door.

Remember

Adverbial phrases tell us when (time), where (place), and how (manner).

Practising your grammar skills

Answer the following questions about adverbials and embedded clauses.

1. Look at the paragraph below with the adverbial phrases and embedded clauses underlined. Notice how these phrases and clauses all need commas.

   Make two lists: one for adverbial phrases and another for embedded clauses.

   <u>Although it was getting dark,</u> Bob, <u>who didn't like the dark,</u> knew he had to go out. It was his turn to lock the henhouse. <u>The night before,</u> a fox had been seen <u>near the garden</u>. The fox, <u>which looked very thin,</u> was obviously hungry. <u>Trying to be quick so he could get the job done as fast as possible,</u> Bob put on his jacket, <u>which he had left by the door,</u> and picked up the big torch.
2. Use the picture on the right to write a paragraph of your own. Include adverbial phrases and embedded *who/which* clauses.
3. Swap paragraphs with a partner. Underline the adverbials and embedded phrases in your partner's writing and hand it back to see if you are right.

Film adaptations

Melanie and Josh are discussing fantasy books and movies. Listen to their opinions.

Listen to the audio for this task:

Understanding

1. What sort of movies are Josh and Melanie discussing?
2. 'In the mind's eye' means seeing something in your imagination. How does this apply to fantasy books and films?
3. Melanie says 'If a director is making a film of a book he – or she – should respect what the author has written.' Find another way to say this in your own words.
4. Josh disagrees with Melanie when she says all fantasy stories are the same. Explain their different points of view.
5. Discuss whether you think some movies are better than the books they come from. Take turns to give your opinions and explain your reasons. Then write down your group's conclusions. Share these ideas with your class.
6. Do you think movies reflect the society they come from? Think of the USA and some of the movies made there. It could be argued that even Hollywood fantasy movies are very American.

Glossary

awesome amazing

I'll grant you that a way of saying 'Yes, all right'

it wasn't remotely realistic not even near to being realistic

Speaking & Listening – working with register

Melanie and Josh are friends talking together. They use an informal register. That means they are speaking using colloquial expressions and interrupting each other. If they had been speaking with a teacher or an adult they did not know, they would have used a more formal register and been more polite about interrupting and disagreeing.

Role-play the following people speaking about the same film and its special effects.

a You are a university professor coming out of a fantasy movie with your colleague, who is also a professor. You did not enjoy the film.

b You are with friends. You thought the film was very good.

c One of you is the professor; one of you is the student. Discuss your opinions of the film's special effects.

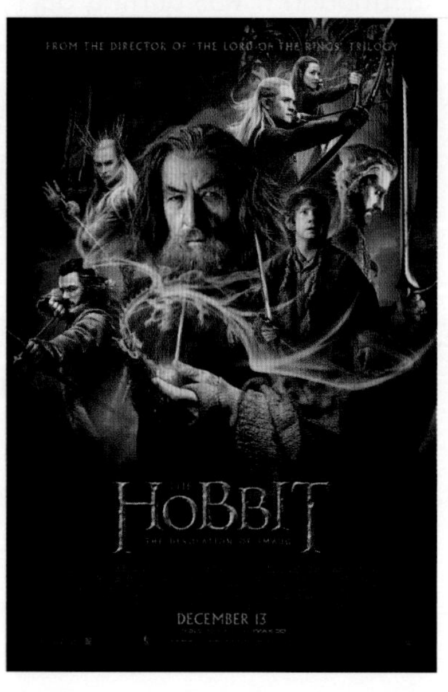

Making a film of a book – practising note-making

Test the skills you have used in this unit on page 12 of the Workbook.

1. Think about a book that you have read that would make a good movie. It can be in any genre.
2. Decide with a partner which book you are going to turn into a film. One of you is the producer in charge of the business side of the film; one of you is the director in charge of what happens on the screen.
3. Write notes on why this book would make a good film. Consider:
   - action
   - intrigue
   - special effects
   - length of the film
   - target audience
   - popularity of genre
   - publicity.
4. Write notes on how you will turn the story into a screenplay. Consider:
   - setting and location (where and when) – the same or different to the book
   - actors who will play main characters
   - actors for secondary characters
   - whether costumes and make-up are for a particular period or to be created
   - what special effects are needed and why
   - what stunts the film will include, if any.
5. When you have finished, share your notes with another pair of students. Carefully read the notes you receive and discuss with your partner similarities and differences to your set of notes.

   Now form a group of four with the pair that received your notes. Have an open-ended discussion about books that would make good films and about good note-making.

Global Perspectives

The movie industry has seen huge change and advancement since the first black and white films were made more than a 100 years ago. One significant development is the use of CGI (computer-generated imagery). Reflect on this development and whether you feel it enhances or detracts from your movie-going experience. What types of movies are popular in your region or country?

Establish

After you complete this section, you will be able to:

- ➔ select a narrative viewpoint that is the most effective for a specific type of fictional story
- ➔ transform your writing to show that you understand different styles and viewpoints
- ➔ create an extended piece of developed and structured story-telling that sustains a reader's interest.

Tip

If you want to develop a single character in depth, a first person narrative is probably the best option.

If you want the reader to infer, or work out some things for themselves, you should probably choose a third person narrative but not one where you as writer seem to know everything that will happen.

Sometimes stories involve imaginary beings in the real world or present the reader with an alternative reality. Characters may be real people or they may seem ordinary but have magic and/or supernatural powers. A good writer can turn a quite ordinary experience into something extra-ordinary.

For example, think about a story that begins with two people waiting for something or someone to arrive. Consider the following:

- who is waiting
- what or who they are waiting for
- the setting – where it happens
- what happens to make the story fantastical or 'not of this world'.

Would such a story function best as a first person narrative or written in the third person? Which would best convey the extraordinary nature of the events, do you think?

This flowchart could be used to generate such a story.

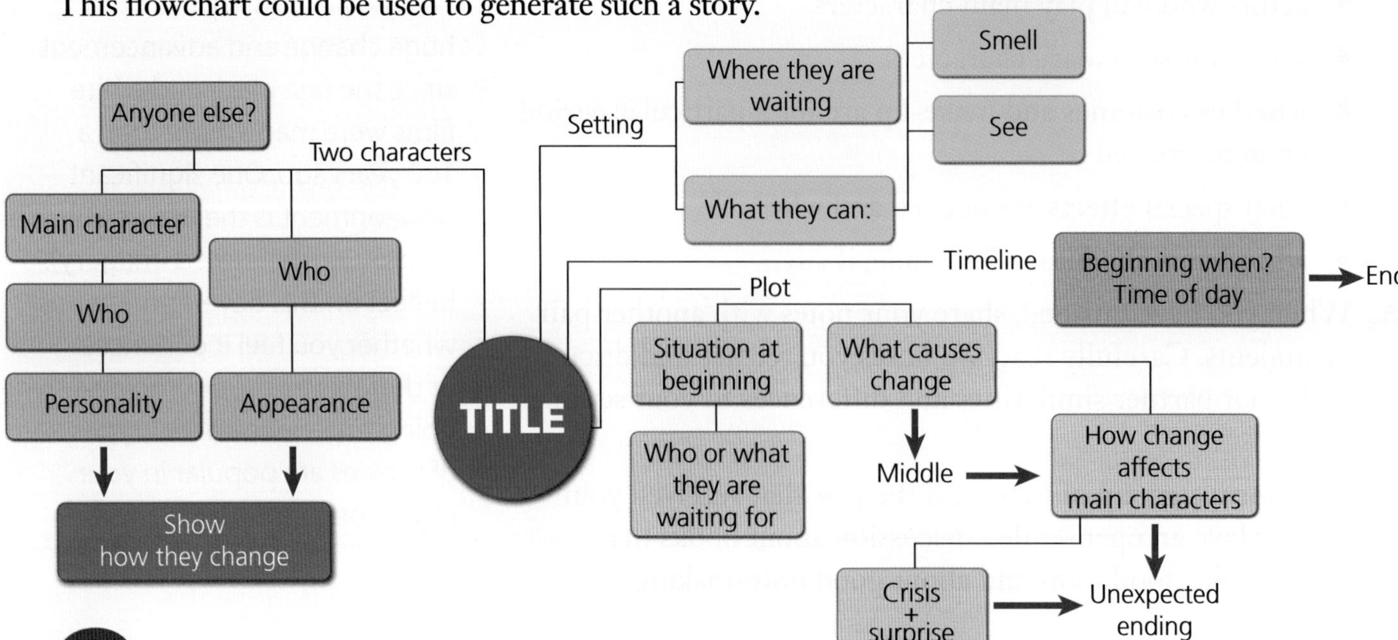

Engage

Analysing the question

Before you even start planning an answer to a writing question, go back and look at the instructions carefully. Check:

➔ the style of writing (fiction or non-fiction) required

➔ if there is a specific audience

➔ if it is a story, whether it is the beginning, the whole story or the end.

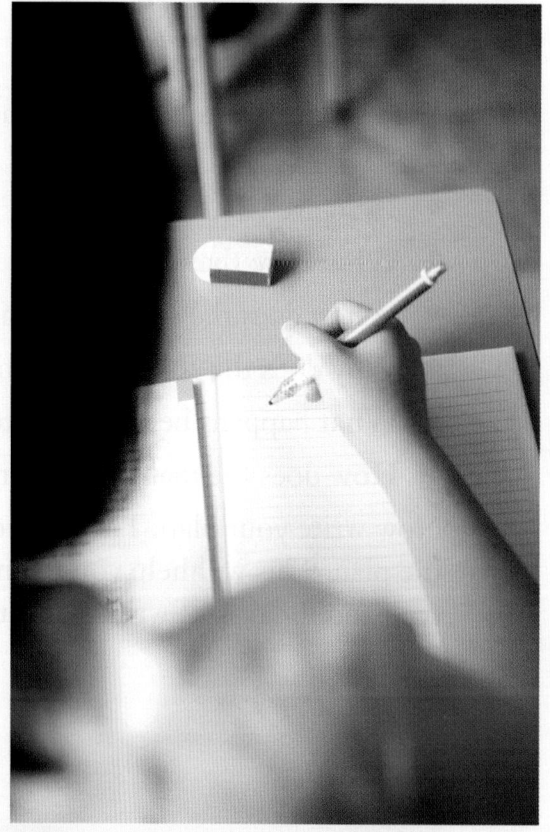

Here is a sample task:

Write a short story where an ordinary event turns into something the reader does not expect.

Consider:

- what ordinary event is taking place
- who is involved
- how the setting and/or the characters are changed by what happens.

The keywords tell you how to answer the question. There are different ways to keyword a question. **Example:**

WHAT I must write – complete story (not just the beginning or the end)

WHAT happens in the story – an ordinary event – Where? When?

Write a short story, where an ordinary event turns into something the reader does not expect.

WHY it happens and the result of the change

HOW it changes – the day, the place and the characters

Planning

When you have finished analysing the question, you can start planning. Keep going back to the question to ensure you are doing what you have been asked.

Have a look at the *wh*– plan on the next page to help you answer this type of question.

The *wh–* planning method

In a six-point *wh–* plan you decide:

Who?	Where?	When?	Why?	What?	How?

You do not have to follow a particular order but you do need to use each word.

- **Who** are your characters?
- **Where** are they?
- **When** does the story take place?
- **Why** does the strange event occur?
- **What** happens before and after the strange event?
- **How** does the main character change during the story?

Now write your plan. There is no need to write the story – just the plan. This will help you to engage with a specific question type and the task of writing creative, controlled fiction.

Tip

Always make a plan for a piece of longer, extended writing. Set the scene, develop the characters and encourage the reader to infer by foreshadowing. Don't forget to include a juicy ending – even if it doesn't solve all of the problems, but poses some more!

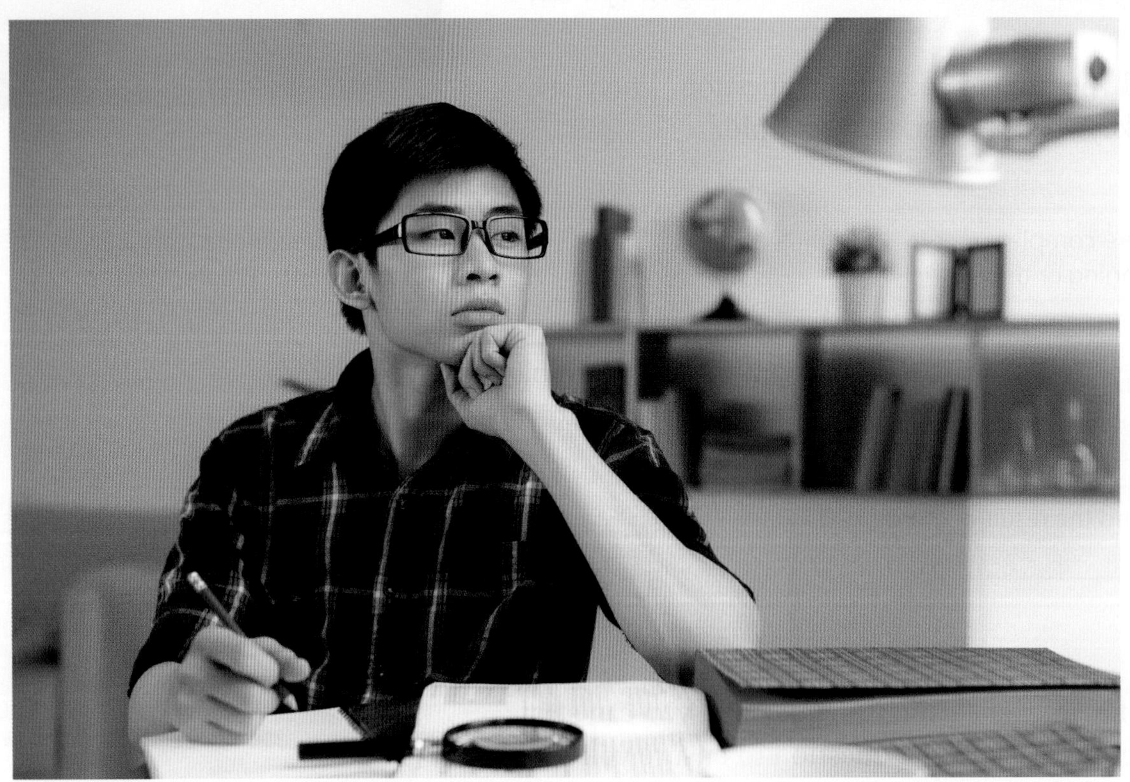

Evaluate

Here are three sample answers responding to the task of writing a short story where an ordinary event turns into something unexpected.

Carry out the following tasks.

1. Read each story and think about:
   - the narrative viewpoint, or narrative voice
   - how the story shows something unexpected
   - how the characters are drawn and whether they change
   - whether the story contains errors in spelling, punctuation or grammar
   - the overall effect of the story – is it convincing, funny, clever, sad, different?
2. When you have read the stories think about the content of each one (plot and characters) and decide which one you prefer. Explain your reasoning.
3. Look at the technical accuracy of each story.
4. Decide which story makes the most sophisticated use of English.
5. Which story asks you to infer the most? Why is inference in story-telling important?

Tip

Irrespective of the narrative viewpoint used, none has any guarantee of accuracy or truth over the other. A first person account could aim to be misleading and a third person account could be entirely based on facts and truth.

Story 1 – The remains of our day

It had the appearance of a normal day. Bright sunshine. A warm, clement and windless morning, not a cloud in sight, with birds and animals in glorious harmony.

The group of friends always met at the same location every weekend, and they would explore the local area on their bikes. Sandeep usually led the way, on his retro 1985 chopper. Followed by Sumitra and Chalaam on their large-wheeled racers. From the perspective of a neutral observer, this peloton of youngsters rushing by erratically in multi-coloured shirts bore the resemblance of a decently average 1980s Hollywood movie.

The *Earth Sectioning* date had arrived, however, and today was not as safe for the teenagers as they believed it to be. How were they to know what might be lurking in the forest beyond? For them, after all, this was a regular outing. The day was not going to end as well as it had begun.

Normality showed itself until late afternoon, by which time the group of five had scoured the perimeter of their imaginary city of Troy. All was calm, no sign of Spartans approaching. The group's code – borrowed from an ancient history lesson at high school – was fully intact. As they sat down in their makeshift camp, they were blissfully ignorant of the external monitoring of the same area, which had been sealed off for a very different, and much more elevated, reason. What happened as dusk arrived was certainly not expected.

Story 2 – School under the sea

I rolled over in bed and slamed my hand down on the alarm botton. Seven o'clock time to get up. Time for school. Another boaring day of lessons and same old same old teachers. Nothing ever changes at my school nothing ever changes in my life.

At nine o'clock I was sitting in Geography next to Shavi, my best friend. He opened the atlas when the teacher handed it to him and gasped. I looked to see why. Shavi had openned it at the page for our country, like the teacher told us to. But our country wasn't there. There was just a space. I starred at the page. We were now under the sea.

Slowly I turned my head and looked out of the window. A fish swimmed by. After that there was a shark. I nuddged Shavi. Look I said. Look!

Shavi opened and closed his mouth exactly like the fish. I pointed to the map on our desk. Look, I said again.

"What are you boys doing? shouted Mr Jones the geography teacher.

"Please sir, I think we're um under watter, sir." I said.

"Don't be ridicilous boy, said Mr Johns.

"Um sir look" said Shavi and he pointed to the window.

There was a huge octapus creeture looking in. I started to laugh because I could see a school of fish then stopped because Mr Joans doesn't like us laughing in his lessons.

Story 3 – The Cabin

The huge purple creature called a Purpon growled as it staggered towards us. I knew I should run but I didn't think I'd be able to escape. Our planet has been taken over by Purpons and Yellons. Yellons are yellow and dangerous, but not as big or strong as Purpons. My friend Tomias said, 'We'd better get out of here.' This was no way to start the day. We started to race across the land where our garden used to be before the Purpons and Yellons started their war. I was in a panic but Tomias was calm. 'Let's get back to the cabin,' he said to me.

Our cabin wasn't far away but it was like hours before we got back inside. Tomias banged our code on the door and Freda let us in. We have to have a code to keep the other kids out because our cabin is really small. It used to be my grandad's garden shed.

Freda looked at us. 'What's happened now?' she asked. Her voice was like a scream. Freda is older than us. She's my sister and sort of behaves like she needs to look after us.

'There's a Purpon – it's coming this way.' Tomias said.

I went to sit on my blanket and tried to get my breath back. I didn't want to think about what would happen if the Purpon found us. We'd be captured or something worst. There weren't many kids left anymore and the Purpons kept getting bigger. You didn't need to be a genius to figure out where the kids were going.

Suddenly the cabin started to shake. The door rattled. Freda screamed. Tomias jumped on his blanket bed and pulled a blanket over his head. The door rattled again then it opened wide and a grey haired head looked in. 'Are you playing in here again?' Grandad said.

Enable

At the beginning of this Assessment workshop, one of your targets was to create an extended piece of fiction writing that has a good structure and sustains a reader's interest. You learned how to approach planning such a piece of writing and what the main elements of successful stories are, including a secure narrative viewpoint.

Now it's your turn to build on your knowledge and skills. But before you do, complete this short exercise to help you develop your narrative writing skills further.

Choose one of the stories you evaluated on pages 21–23 and write a shorter version of it using a different narrative voice. You could experiment with one of these:

- first person
- second person
- using only dialogue
- third person omniscient
- third person not fully omniscient.

Tip

With this type of extended writing, you will be expected to write two to three sides of A4 lined paper (six to nine paragraphs) in about 30 minutes. Plan your paragraphs carefully so that each flows smoothly and links to the next one.

Tip

Once you have decided on a narrative voice, it's best to remain consistent and stay in that voice to avoid confusing the reader. It is possible, for example, to write a novel entirely in the second person. Such novels do exist, even though they are rare and unusual.

Follow up – writing a story

Write your answer to the following task.

Read the following opening to a story.

Continue the story, choosing your own title.

Spend 30 minutes writing, after you have made your plan.

> Sandeep wasn't sure what had made him check the perimeter again – this was the first time in many visits to the forest that he had felt the need to do that – but when he saw the bright lights in the distance, and what came out of the mist, he froze in silence.
>
> "Hey, you there, stay exactly where you are."

You should consider:

- who issued the command to stay put, describing the scene in detail
- what happened when Sandeep was met
- what happened next and what happened to Sandeep's friends waiting at the base camp.

When you have finished, discuss your story with your teacher.

2 Discovering the past

In this unit, you will engage with the past and what we can learn from it. You will read about the discovery of a new species of dinosaur, enjoy how an American family make a startling discovery in an old English house, and study the remains of a king whose skeleton was found in a parking lot! You will also practise summary writing on the theme of new discoveries about sleeping habits.

And in doing all that, you will be practising these key skills:

Speaking & Listening

- Take up the roles of people who study the ancient past, demonstrating some of their expertise.
- Act out a scary dramatic scene to increase your confidence in performing drama.

Writing

- Create a diary entry about working on an archaeological dig, manipulating content to ensure impact on your audience.
- Use the organisational features of summary writing to show how sleeping patterns can affect sports performance.

Reading

- Scan a newspaper article to analyse the implications of explicit information about the discovery of a new species of dinosaur.
- Analyse how a dramatist uses a combination of irony and humour to enhance intended meaning in a scene.

Assessment workshop

You will gain practice in the key skill of comparing two extended texts with a similar topic or theme. You will note similarities and differences, make appropriate notes and write a summary based on two texts.

Thinking time

1. Do you think a scientist or historian sees things differently from other people?
2. Serendipity is finding something you didn't know you were looking for. Has this ever happened to you? Have any scientific discoveries been accidental?
3. Do you think there is anything left to discover?

"Discovery consists of seeing what everybody has seen and thinking what nobody has thought."
Albert von Szent-Györgyi

Did you know the word serendipity comes from an old fairy tale, The Three Princes of Serendip, in which the characters constantly discovered things they were not seeking?

Uncovering the past

Most inventions are improvements on previous ideas or items, and the world is constantly developing and changing, but knowing about the future depends on knowing about the past. For this we need historians and scientists, such as palaeontologists and archaeologists, who discover the past and solve ancient mysteries.

Palaeontology is the study of the history of life on Earth as reflected in fossils in the Earth's crust. It involves physics, chemistry, biology and geology. Palaeontologists look for clues to what happened in the very distant past to help us understand how the Earth developed and what may happen next.

Archaeology is the study of what remains of past civilisations. This involves examining geographical sites and ancient buildings to learn who lived there and how they lived. Archaeologists know about geography, geology, anthropology (the study of humans and their customs) and folklore.

Some of these scientists go on digs, seeking the answers to age-old mysteries that affect our current thinking and could affect the future, such as: Why did dinosaurs become extinct? Could it happen to us?

Speaking & Listening – studying the past

Read the text about people who search for the past. Then work with a partner to answer the questions.

1. Who studies the distant prehistoric past and who looks at the ruins of buildings?
2. One of you is a palaeontologist, the other an archaeologist. Make notes about your job, then tell your partner about it. Include what you do, what you have studied and what you want to find.
3. Discuss how your jobs are similar and how they differ.

 A spectacular discovery

This extract from a newspaper article describes finding a new type of dinosaur.

Battleship beast: colossal dinosaur skeleton found in southern Patagonia

By Ian Sample, Science Editor

Dreadnoughtus schrani, unearthed in Argentina, is the most complete skeleton of a plant-eating titanosaur recovered anywhere in the world.

The spectacular remains of one of the largest beasts ever to walk the planet have been unearthed by fossil hunters in southern Patagonia.

The unique **haul** of bones includes a metre-wide neck vertebra, a thigh bone that stands as tall as a man and ribs the size of planks, representing the most complete skeleton of a colossal plant-eating titanosaur recovered anywhere in the world.

The new species was so enormous that researchers named it *Dreadnoughtus schrani* after the dreadnought battleships of the early 20th century on the grounds that it would fear nothing that crossed its path.

From measurements of the bones, scientists worked out that *Dreadnoughtus* reached 26 metres from snout to tail, making it the largest land animal for which an accurate body mass can be calculated.

The colossal *Dreadnoughtus* lived around 77 million years ago in a temperate forest at the southern tip of South America. Its bodyweight equates to as many as a dozen African elephants or more than seven of

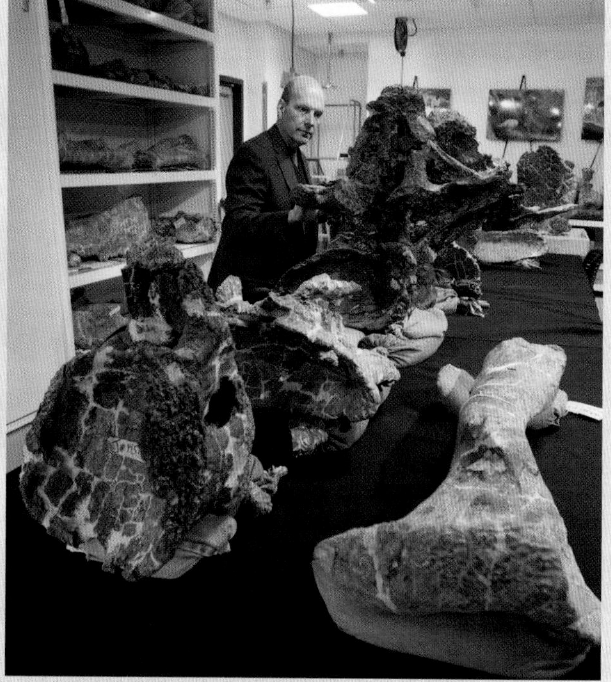

the *Tyrannosaurs rex* species, according to Kenneth Lacorvara, a palaeontologist at Drexel University in Philadelphia. (…)

Lacorvara caught a first glimpse of the remains during a field trip to the **stunning** but barren **scrubland** of southern Patagonia in 2005. What appeared to be a small collection of bones soon became an extensive haul of more than 100 bone fragments, exquisitely well preserved when the animal apparently drowned in quicksand.

Though staggering in its dimensions, close inspection of the bones revealed that the animal was not fully grown when it died. "That was a real shock to us," Lacorvara told *The Guardian (...)*.

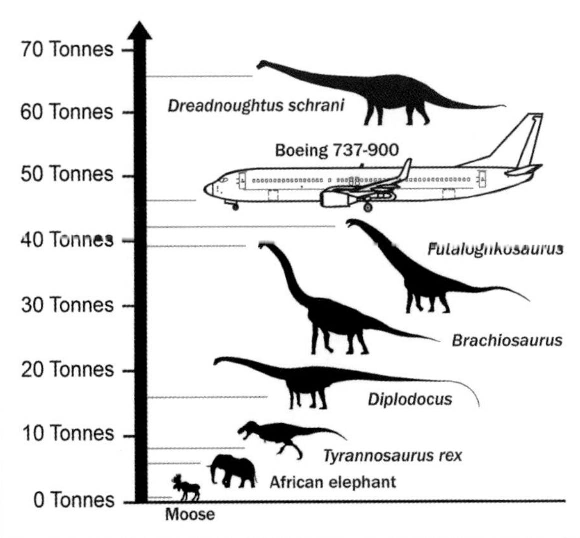

Size and weight of the Dreadnoughtus schrani *compared to other species. This animal was heavier than a Boeing 737*

The site lies around 62 miles (100 km) off the power grid and four hours' drive from the nearest town. "I've spent a total of about a year living in my tent next to this dinosaur. We live very simply down there. We eat crackers for breakfast, a can of tuna and a piece of cheese for lunch, and every night we have a piece of meat on a stick," Lacorvara said. "Every couple of weeks we make a **foray** into town for food and showers."

In the late Cretaceous period, the site was a mixed forest of conifers and broad-leafed trees cut through by **meandering** waterways. The rivers were **prone** to flooding, and the sudden surge of water would have turned surrounding flood plains into sinking sand. The *Dreadnoughtus* was apparently in the wrong place at the wrong time. "Shortly after these individuals died, or as they died, they were buried quickly and deeply in what was essentially quicksand. That led to the high number of bones and the **exquisite** preservation," Lacorvara said. (...)

From an article in the UK newspaper, *The Guardian, 4 July 2014*

Word cloud

exquisite	**prone**
foray	**scrubland**
haul	**stunning**
meandering	

Understanding

Answer the following questions using information from the article.

1. a What name has been given to the dinosaur?

b Why was it given this name?

c What type of dinosaur was it?

2. Explain in your own words how the titanosaur may have died, then find a quotation in the article (words or a phrase) to support your answer.

Global Perspectives

Reflect on these two elements: that the dinosaur was not yet fully grown and what led to dinosaurs perishing. It is likely that humans were not involved. However, the relationship between humans and other species is arguably more at risk today than ever in our entire history on the planet.

3. How does the area where the skeleton was found differ from how it used to be when the dinosaur lived there? Find words and phrases in the article to support your answer.
4. How does the writer try to help the reader understand how big the titanosaur is? Give two examples from the article.
5. What sort of life has the palaeontologist led during the dig? Think about the location of the dig and how this affected Lacorvara's lifestyle.
6. Think only about the natural world and planet Earth. What would be a fantastic new discovery? It could be on land, in the oceans or perhaps on the Arctic ice fields. How would you like to be involved in such a discovery?

Word builder

Write a diary entry.

Imagine it is the day on which the 100th bone has been found. You are a palaeontology student who has been working on the dig. Describe your feelings as you realise there are now enough bones to recreate the vast skeleton of the titanosaur. Write your thoughts in your diary. Use all of the words from the Word cloud. Start with the word *Eureka!*

Include:

- what life on the dig in Patagonia has been like
- something about your daily routine
- the moment you realised that your team had found the 100th bone
- what finding this bone means.

Developing your language – direct and reported speech

Direct speech uses inverted commas. Reported speech does not have inverted commas and is often introduced by *that*.

Examples:

Direct speech: *"The size of the beast was a complete surprise," Jose Esquina, a history student, told us.*

Reported speech: *Jose Esquina, a history student, told us that the size of the beast was a complete surprise.*

1. Although the dimensions of the dinosaur were staggering, close inspection of the bones revealed that the animal was not fully grown when it died. "That was a real shock to us," Lacorvara told *The Guardian* newspaper's reporter.

   You are a journalist reporting on the discovery. Rewrite the paragraph in your own words, using reported speech.
2. Write a conversation between Monica and Hanni about the discovery of *Dreadnaughtus schrani*. Monica thinks it is fascinating; Hanni thinks it is a waste of time and money. Include where the discovery was made and who made it.
3. Write a paragraph reporting on what Hanni said in the conversation. Start like this: *Hanni believes searching for the past is a waste of time. He said . . .*
4. How many words do you know to describe something enormous?
   - **a** Make a list of ways to say something is very big.
   - **b** Use a dictionary to find the meaning and origin of the word *colossal*.
   - **c** Use your words in direct speech to report the sighting of the largest ever mammal in the ocean. It may be a new species.

Remember

The article about *Dreadnoughtus schrani* on pages 28–29 was written for a daily newspaper. Though this important and exciting discovery was made by highly qualified scientists, the language of the article is easy to understand. It uses familiar comparisons to help us imagine the creature's colossal size.

 A dreadful discovery

Read the following scenes based on 'The Canterville Ghost' by Oscar Wilde. Examine how Wilde uses comedy.

Scene 1 *Lord Canterville is selling his ancestral family home to an American, Mr Otis, whose family immediately moves in.*

Lord Canterville: I ought to tell you, we haven't actually wanted to live here since my great-grandaunt … felt the skeleton hands of Sir Simon on her shoulders.

Mr Otis: My Lord, I am happy to pay for all furniture and fittings – including your family ghost – if he exists.

Lord Canterville: Oh he exists, sir! Be warned! And he always appears before a death in the family.

Mr Otis: So does a doctor, Lord Canterville. I come from a modern country where we have everything money can buy. Believe me, if there were such a thing as a ghost, we'd have one. Do you expect me to pay more for the pleasure of having a ghost on the premises?

Lord Canterville: No, good heavens, no! Well, if you don't mind taking on Sir Simon, I'm happy to conclude the sale. But please remember, I did warn you.

Mr Otis: I understand, sir. However, there is no such thing as a ghost, and *if* Sir Simon *is* here, I will be forced to charge him rent.

Scene 2 *Sir Simon, in a white sheet, looks at a pot of cleaning fluid and a paint box left open on a table. His portrait is on the floor and the bloodstain has gone from the rug.*

Sir Simon: Who do these people think they are? They walk in here like they own the place, leave their possessions wherever they like and… remove my portrait *[puts it back on the wall]*… *and* remove my bloodstain. And that's just their first day! I've kept this bloodstain here for 300 years … and I'm certainly not going to let a few Americans ruin it – or my ghostly reputation – now. These people must go! *[Lets out a terrifying moan and disappears]*.

Glossary

dock his wages deduct money for breaking the coffee cup

furniture and fittings everything in the house, including rugs and curtains

Scene 3 *Next morning at breakfast.*

Washington Otis [son]: Everyone sleep well last night? Oh, look, the bloodstain is back. I guess there is a ghost after all.

Virginia Otis [daughter] opens her paint box.

Virginia Otis: That's odd; my brick red paint has all gone.

James, the butler, enters with a tray of coffee and cups.

Mrs Otis: Look, the portrait of that horrid Sir Simon fellow is back on my wall! James, did you do that?

James: The portrait *[drops tray]*... agh! *[faints]*

Washington: Oh dear, the butler has fainted. Remember to dock his wages, Mother.

Developing your language – using humour

1. Oscar Wilde uses the character of Mr Otis to make the reader smile. Can you identify how?
2. In his first words, Mr Otis downgrades Sir Simon to amuse himself. How does he do this?
3. A doctor doesn't always appear before a death. Is Mr Otis trying to be funny in line 11?
4. In line 22, how is the idea of paying rent humorous?
5. What is the playwright really doing in his portrayal of Mr Otis?

Speaking & Listening – a dramatic scene

Sir Simon reappears late the next night. A tremendous crash brings everyone rushing downstairs to discover an old suit of armour has fallen and Sir Simon is sitting rubbing his knees. He then walks through the family and disappears. Mr Otis's children decide to trap Sir Simon.

Write another scene with Sir Simon and the children, describing their plan to trap Sir Simon.

1. Write your scene in the form of a playscript.
2. Act out your playscript in groups.
3. Compare the different ways that have been found to trap the ghost.

Combining words

Making old words into new words

We often put two words together to create a new meaning, for example: *fossil* + *hunter* = someone who hunts for fossils.

We do this for new ideas and inventions. For example: *skate* + *board* = *skateboard*

Look at the words below, which are all associated with modern sports. How many words can you make by mixing and matching words from each of the two boxes? Write a list. You can use each word more than once.

The first one has been done for you: *windsurfer*.

wind roller skate ice snow kite

hockey surfer blade rink skate board

New words – portmanteau words

The term *portmanteau word* comes from Lewis Carroll's *Through the Looking Glass*, when Humpty Dumpty explains to Alice, "You see it's like a portmanteau — there are two meanings packed up into one word."

A portmanteau is a suitcase that has two separate sections. The picture illustrates how we make new words for new ideas, inventions or discoveries using words we already know.

titan + dinosaur = titanosaur
fog + smoke = smog
breakfast + lunch = brunch

Answer the following questions.

1. Join the two words together to make a portmanteau word:
   - **a** *web* + *log* =
   - **b** *parachute* + *trooper* =
   - **c** *guess* + *estimate* =
   - **c** *helicopter* + *ski* =
2. Work with a partner to invent some portmanteau words of your own for the following categories:
   - sport
   - entertainment
   - school
   - food
   - transport.

Remember

Sometimes we use a hyphen when we join two or more words together. Examples are *close-up, brother-in-law* and *man-of-war* (a type of battleship). To make these nouns plural, you sometimes need to change the first part: *brothers*-in-law, *men*-of war.

Prepositions

Little words that do a lot

Prepositions give us information about time and place.

The lighthouse keeper sat **in** his chair **throughout** the night, staring **at** the sky **through** his small window.

Words that are prepositions can also act as adverbs, but a preposition requires an object and an adverb does not.

Examples:

If you want to see the moonlight, go ***outside****.*	**outside** = adverb
There was a long queue ***outside*** *the cinema.*	**outside** = preposition

Prepositions usually come before nouns and noun phrases. For example:

The palaeontologists camped ***beside*** *the dig.*

The Dreadnoughtus *was* ***in*** *the wrong place* ***at*** *the wrong time.*

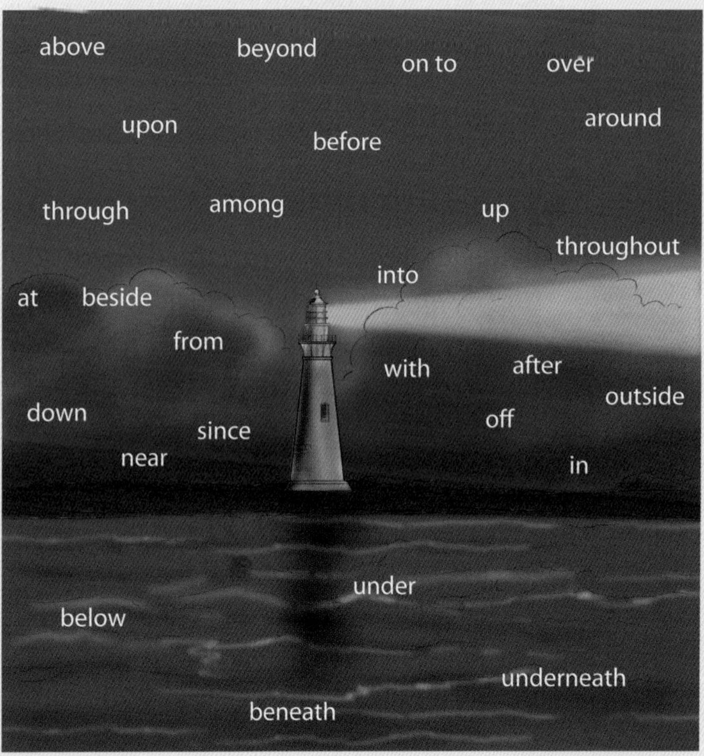

Prepositional phrases

A prepositional phrase is made up of the preposition, its object and associated adjectives or adverbs.

We use prepositional phrases for many purposes:

- as adverbials of time and place
- with a noun phrase
- to show who did something
- after certain verbs, nouns and adjectives.

Example:

The student, <u>who was ***in** the library* looking **for** information **on** fossils</u>, was looking ***through*** *an old journal* the librarian had found <u>*in a box **under** his desk*</u>.

Answer the following questions.

1. Write a sentence about where you are now and underline the prepositions and/or prepositional phrase.
2. Write two sentences about what you did last weekend and ask a partner to find the prepositions and/or prepositional phrases.
3. Write a short paragraph about finding something surprising in your grandmother's cupboard. Include as many prepositions and prepositional phrases as you can.

Richard III, king of England

Read this blog post about finding the skeleton of Richard III, an English king, under a car park. Then listen to a radio news broadcast about it.

Discuss how the discovery affects what people know about a king who is supposed to have murdered his nephews and who died in battle in 1485.

The skeleton identified as King Richard III

The king under the car park

I've been reading about the discovery of the much-hated (or misunderstood) King Richard III. His skeleton was located under a car park in Leicestershire, England. Richard III, a Plantagenet, was the last monarch of the House of York, and the last English king to die in battle.

The skeleton, with a slightly curved spine, has now been examined and scientists have proved its identity through DNA analysis of a 17th-generation Plantagenet descendant. It is fascinating, the power of modern science to play historical detective. But what I'd like to know is: did Richard really murder his young nephews in the Tower of London?

In his play *Richard III*, Shakespeare created a hideous, horrible villain that people actually believe in. But as far as I know, when Edward IV died in April 1483 (a hundred years before Shakespeare's play) Richard *did* escort his nephew, 12-year-old Edward V to the Tower of London, where he was joined by his little brother, and the two young princes never appeared again. At the time, it was rumoured they'd been murdered by Richard so he could be king. So Shakespeare's version could be true.

Listen to the audio for this task:

Glossary

carbon dated when organic objects have been dated using measurements of the amount of radio carbon they contain

historical sources original documents and evidence from the period

osteo-archaeologist an archaeologist specialising in bones

Plantagenet a ruling English family of the House of York

potentially fatal capable of killing

rigorous study a careful and thorough examination

Understanding

Answer the following questions.

1. Who was the real Richard III?
2. What does the discovery prove about how Shakespeare portrayed the king?
3. How has modern science been used to identify the skeleton found in Leicester?
4. The archaeologist Richard Buckley said the bones had been subjected to a 'rigorous study'. Why do you think it was so important to study the skeleton?
5. Why, in your opinion, do historians need to look at historical sources again in this case?
6. Imagine you are an investigative reporter and you have just uncovered something which proves a previous historical event to be false or very inaccurate. Write your news report, which can be two minutes long.

A portrait of Richard III

monarch
portrayed
reins (of power)
rumours

Word builder

1. The words and expressions in the Word cloud come from the news broadcast. Match each one with its meaning.

monarch	made out to be
reins of power	the ruler of the country
rumours	control of the country
portrayed	tittle-tattle

2. Why do you think the people who wrote the news about the discovery of the king's skeleton used the words in the Word cloud and not the other words and expressions in the box above?
3. Use information from the blog and the news broadcast to write a paragraph on the discovery for an international newspaper. Use words and expressions from the Glossary and Word cloud. Write in a formal, informative style.
4. When you have finished, ask a partner to read out your paragraph in a formal style.

Global Perspectives

The world has some major and contrasting belief systems. Kings and queens of England, for example, are highly regarded in the national culture. Some people believe that a monarchy provides a solid basis for government and brings many benefits. Analyse one of your local or national belief systems. Does it merge with global systems?

Writing a summary

Read this blog article about the discovery that the more you sleep, the better you can make split-second decisions.

What time is bedtime?

Lately, I've been getting worried about our twins' bedtime and lack of sleep. It's common knowledge that most teenagers don't get enough sleep. Gloria, who has a wide social network, is in constant contact with her friends; Tobias is a grade A achiever and has to stay top of the class. So in one way or another, these two kids are just too busy to sleep. But they need sleep, especially as the one thing they have in common is playing competition-level tennis.

As a doctor, I know that not getting enough sleep can build into a serious sleep deficit. Teenagers with a sleep deficit find it hard to concentrate or do any form of academic work effectively. They can also have emotional problems, and it seriously affects sports performance.

Research shows that adolescents need about nine hours' sleep a night. That means, ideally, a teenager who wakes up to prepare for school at 7 a.m. should go to bed around ten o'clock at night. Studies show, however, that many teens have trouble falling asleep that early. It's not because they don't want to sleep; it's because their brains are working later in the evening and they simply aren't ready for bed. During adolescence, the body's biological clock is reset, telling a teenager to fall asleep later at night and wake up later in the morning than they did when they were younger.

As a sports' doctor, I also know most young athletes live for their sport. In addition to healthy eating, they need to think about healthy sleeping. Sleep plays a major role in athletic performance and competition results. The quality and amount of sleep athletes get is often *the key* to winning. If sleep is cut short, the body doesn't have time to rest, create memory and release hormones. A study in the journal *Sleep* confirms the role of a good night's slumber in athletics and team sports. There is a serious decline in split-second decision-making following a poor night's sleep, which could be catastrophic for tennis singles or team players alike. Results also show increased accuracy in well-rested subjects. Good hydration and the right diet are only part of training and recovery. Good sleep is vital to prevent the possibility of fatigue, low energy and poor focus at game time. It may also help recovery after the game.

Directed summaries

The type of summary you will be asked to write is a directed summary. This means you will be given a specific area to summarise. For example, you might be asked to write a summary with the direction: parents' concerns about teenagers' sleeping patterns.

Can you think of two or three other directions that could be given for a directed summary about this article?

Glossary

hydration drinking enough water

sleep deficit the number of hours needed to catch up on sleep

slumber peaceful sleep

WB

Test the skills you have used in this unit on page 21 of the Workbook.

Writing a summary

Write a summary of up to 100 words on why a good night's sleep is important for success in sports performance. Before you start your summary, look at the plan below to help you.

Preparing for summary questions

1. Find key words in the question. Ask: Do I need all the information in the text or just some of it?
2. Read the text again carefully and identify the relevant phrases, sentences or paragraph(s) for your summary.
3. Look at the question again. Check that you are not including unnecessary details.

Writing your summary

1. Write your summary, in your own words as far as possible.
2. Count the words and make changes if necessary.
3. Proofread your final summary and correct any spelling and/or punctuation mistakes.

Establish

After you complete this section, you will be able to:

- ➔ read texts on the same theme but from different sources
- ➔ compare and contrast the texts, identifying their similarities and differences
- ➔ synthesise information from the texts in an extended written response.

Tip

When reading a text you are intending to summarise, scan for and underline the key details or facts that appear to be linked together.

Here are two extracts about the discovery of prehistoric cave paintings and how modern science is helping to preserve them.

Text A

This is an extract from 'Barbara's blog'.

Cave holidays in Spain

This summer I've been in two caves in northern Spain looking at prehistoric artwork.

El Castillo Cave

The paintings on the walls of El Castillo Cave have been dated at more than 40 000 years old. It contains what might be the oldest cave art in the world! … Some scientists think the paintings were done by Neanderthals.

As you walk through the cave, you see rows of red hand-prints and patterns of dots on the walls. There are also really detailed drawings of animals, including horses, deer, bison, goats, mammoths and dogs. What impressed me most were the hand prints. They look small – smaller than mine, that is. Obviously we weren't allowed to touch the paintings but I waved one of my hands in front of the low light from the torches to compare. Perhaps the prints were done by young children.

Altamira Cave

In Altamira Cave, there are images of bison that show whoever painted them had very impressive art skills because they used the shape of the cave walls, the curves and contours, to make the bison appear three-dimensional. You can almost see them moving, galloping across the hills. There are also depictions of goats, horses, female deer and wild boar, as well as some abstract shapes, red spots and hand prints. This cave is not actually open to the public, but we explored an amazing replica at the Altamira Museum. Not the same as the real thing in El Castillo, though…

Text B

This is an extract from an article about the discovery of ancient paintings in a cave in Wales.

Tip

Make a mental note of what appears to be different in the second text. What details are added? Is the writing style different?

Stone Age wall paintings found in a cave in Wales

The Welsh cave system had been known about for decades and local school children visited the upper levels on field trips. It wasn't until 1998 that the discovery of wall paintings was made.

Alana Thomas and her team of experts had been working on making the upper levels more stable, as local people had noticed that the rock floor was thinning out. Alana was the first to see what the team had exposed, late one Sunday evening in autumn. "It was like looking at a hologram. As if we weren't actually looking at a real cave, but a three-dimensional image made by lasers. It smelled so fresh."

They had found a huge secondary cave covered with prehistoric paintings of animals: horses, mammoths and hippopotamuses, looking as fresh as they were painted thousands of years ago during the Stone Age. It soon became necessary to cordon off the find to prevent any damage to the art vault that was now unhidden.

It took years and substantial investment by the government to protect this new site. However, there was always going to be a challenge – how to make these cave paintings accessible to people.

In 2002, the solution was found. A full-size replica was commissioned by the government, involving officials, geologists and artists. There was a tough task ahead – to recreate the cave 10 km away so that people could still see the extent to which the Stone Age artists had been active.

Hundreds of paintings would feature, with mammoths among the largest creatures. Handprints and carvings were also re-created. The new location would mimic the depths and features of the original find, so that viewers would feel the cold, the humidity and the atmosphere in which the Stone Age artists had operated.

The geologists theorised how the original cave work had stayed so remarkably fresh. It took the team of scientists a few months' research and they eventually found the reason. A rockslide, which must have occurred many thousands of years ago, had effectively sealed off the site to outside impediments.

Engage

Answer the following questions.

1. Which text is written in the most informal style and why?
2. Use Text A to answer the following questions.
   - **a** Finish the following sentence, including a colon in your description.

     In El Castillo cave she saw....
   - **b** The writer says she liked one cave more than another. Which cave did she prefer? Explain why.
   - **c** Who did the writer think might have been responsible for the prints in El Castillo Cave?
3. Use Text B to answer these questions about the discovery of the cave in Wales.
   - **a** How did Alana Thomas and her team find the cave?
   - **b** What did the Stone Age artists paint?
   - **c** How were the paintings preserved for so many years?
4. Make some notes about each text. You can only make four notes on each one, so look for the main points.
5. Now think about how these two accounts of discoveries in caves are different. Note down as many main differences as you can.

Tip

When making notes, only include details that are present in the text. It's not a good idea to infer a note, i.e to add your own note!

Evaluate

Read the following three attempts at 50-word summaries of what visitors can see in the replica of the original cave in Wales.

A *In the replica visitors can see: painted animals and hand prints from the cave walls. There are hundred paints of animals. They have copied the animals that are dead now like the mamoth. They have also made the same temeperature and smell.*

B *The replica cave shows hundreds of paintings copied from the real cave. that was like an art-gallery. Visitors get the experience as if they are in a real cave even if it's a replica. Scientists made the same atmosphere.*

c In the reproduction visitors can see and feel what it was like in the real prehistoric cave. There are hundreds of painted animals, carvings and hand prints. The replica also has the same sort of atmosfere as the real cave; damp humidity.

Using these bullet points to help you, think about which summary is best.

- The answer does not repeat words or phrases unless necessary.
- The answer is not over the word limit.
- The sentences flow together well.
- The answer contains the relevant information.
- The answer does not contain irrelevant information.
- The summary is mostly written in the writer's own words.
- The spelling is correct.
- There are only minor spelling mistakes.
- The grammar and punctuation are correct.

Tip

When writing longer summaries, it is useful to think about the summary as a series of notes that you then link together with your own words and a good range of conjunctions.

Enable

At the beginning of this Assessment workshop, one of your targets was to synthesise information from two texts with a similar theme.

Read the new extract about caves on the next page.

Trapped in Tham Luang Nang Non Cave

In the summer months of 2018, a cave rescue saved the lives of members of a junior football team who were trapped inside the Tham Luang Nang Non Cave in Chiang Rai Province, Thailand. Twelve members of the team, aged 11–16, and their 25-year-old assistant coach entered the cave on 23 June after football practice. Shortly afterwards, heavy rains partially flooded the large cave network, blocking their way out.

Efforts to locate the group were hampered by rising water levels and strong currents, and no contact could be made for more than a week. The rescue effort grew into a massive operation which was covered by the global media. On 2 July, after advancing through numerous narrow passages and muddy waters, two British divers found the group alive on an elevated rock about 4 kilometres from the entrance to the cave.

International and Thai rescue organisers discussed various options for getting the group to safety. Options included whether to teach them basic diving skills to enable their early rescue; to wait until a new entrance was found or drilled; or to wait for the floodwaters to subside at the end of the monsoon season, which would be months later. After days of pumping water from the cave system and a

respite from rain, the rescue teams wanted to act before the next monsoon rain, which was expected to bring significant additional rainfall and was predicted to start around 11 July. That would effectively seal the cave and conserve its contents.

Between 8 and 10 July, all 12 of the boys and their coach were rescued from the cave by an international team. When it comes to caves, teamwork is essential.

The rescue effort involved over 10,000 people, including more than 100 divers, many rescue workers, representatives from about 100 governmental agencies, 900 police officers and 2,000 soldiers. It required ten police helicopters, seven ambulances, more than 700 diving cylinders and the pumping of more than a billion litres of water from the caves.

Caves are clearly awe-inspiring and wonderful but can also be dangerous places.

1. What do you think Alana Thomas's team and the boys from the Thai football team have in common? Try to come up with three things they have in common.

Tip

Be careful about prior knowledge. You may well remember the escapades of the Thai junior football team. It's important to use only information from the texts and not to assume your general knowledge is needed, or accurate.

2. Compare and contrast the Welsh and Thai caves, and the experiences of the two teams involved. Complete the table with some bullet point notes. One similarity and one difference have been given as examples.

Similarities	Differences
• Both caves are immense, in large networks, with numerous tunnels	• Far more people (thousands) were involved in the Thai caving operation

Follow up – writing an article

Using information from both extracts (on the Welsh and Thai caves), your own words and some of your own ideas, respond to the following task.

Write an article that will feature in an outdoor activity magazine about the wonders and dangers of exploring caves.

You should consider:

- the attractive elements and pleasures of caves and exploring them
- what you have learned about caves and caving from both extracts
- the advice you would give to a team about to set off on a caving expedition
- whether you would enjoy going deep into a cave.

You should aim to write about 200 words.

Tip

When you are synthesising, try to use discourse markers to compare and contrast. For example:

On the one hand exploring caves can be very exciting, but on the other hand you should always take full precautions to ensure safety at all times.

Good use of discourse markers helps the reader navigate through your writing.

When you have finished, discuss your article with your teacher.

3 Influencers

In this unit, you will meet people who have had a strong influence, either intentionally or as a result of their prominence. You will read about the effect the famous beauty Helen had on the inhabitants of two ancient cities, learn about the philanthropic work of a fashion model, and listen to a discussion about charisma and how it can be used to influence others. You will create a proposal for a new drama series with two influential main characters.

And in doing all that, you will be practising these key skills:

Speaking & Listening

- Take part in a group discussion about what makes some people well known, famous and influential.
- Role-play an interview, noting how the two roles of host and guest interact and differ.

Writing

- Adopt the point of view of a main character and re-write an account from their perspective.
- Integrate dramatic structure, dialogue and sub-plots into a larger theme.

Reading

- Engage with an account of a ten-year war that laid siege to the city of Troy, noting the key elements of a synopsis.
- Evaluate the contributions made by a philanthropist – a fashion model who went on to found a school and a football academy.

Assessment workshop

You will gain practice in the key assessment skill of summarising, by reading a long summary of an account of the arrest of an infamous criminal and refining your skills of collating and synthesis. You will learn how to retain the important content and how to recognise the language of summarising.

Thinking time

1. 'Handsome is as handsome does.' People should be judged by what they do, not what they look like. Do you agree?
2. If beauty lies only 'in the eyes of the beholder', why is social media full of images of 'beautiful people'?
3. Jon Bon Jovi is an American singer-songwriter, record producer, philanthropist and actor. His albums have sold over 130 million worldwide and he has been ranked at 50 on *Billboard* magazine's 'Power 100' (a ranking of 'the most powerful and influential people in the music business'), but what does his quotation tell you about his personality and his success?

"Beauty lies in the eyes of the beholder."
Plato

Handsome is as handsome does.

"Success is falling nine times and getting up ten."
Jon Bon Jovi

Speaking & Listening – qualities for success

1. Can you identify the people below? If not, look at what they are doing. Can you think of other well-known people who are successful in similar roles?
2. Decide which of the personality traits or qualities listed on the right helped them to achieve their success.
3. Which traits or qualities, if any, have *not* been used? Say why.

determination	skill
self-confidence	talent
passion	reliability
imagination	humility
self-interest	persistence
vision	single-mindedness
charisma	arrogance
self-discipline	moodiness

'The face that launch'd a thousand ships'

The Greek myth of Helen of Troy is thousands of years old and has fame very much at its heart.

Tyndareus, King of Sparta, had a daughter, Helen, whose beauty was **renowned** throughout the isles of Greece and beyond. When the time came for Helen to marry, many chiefs and kings came to Sparta to beg for her hand. This put Tyndareus' kingdom in **jeopardy**. Helen could only choose one man, meaning those who were rejected might cause trouble. To avoid this, Tyndareus insisted Helen's **suitors** agree to a 'suitors' oath': that they would come to the aid of whoever won her, should the need arise. Helen eventually chose Menelaus.

During this time, in Troy (also called Ilium) three immortal goddesses decided the most handsome man on Earth was Paris, Prince of Troy, and demanded he decide which of them was the loveliest. Paris, who had a keen eye for beauty, could not decide so, quietly, each of the divine contestants offered him a bribe. Athena offered success in battle; Hera offered rule over Asia; Aphrodite promised him the most beautiful mortal woman as his wife. Paris, who some say knew all about Helen of Sparta, chose Aphrodite (and her bribe). Whether Paris knew Helen was now married or not, his eye for beauty started the Trojan War.

Paris crossed the sea and became the guest of Helen and Menelaus, who had inherited the kingdom of Sparta. Shortly after, Menelaus left for Crete, and Helen was alone with their good-looking guest. The next we are told, Paris fled with Helen and her priceless jewels back to Troy.

When Menelaus heard of the betrayal, he called in the 'suitors' oath' and raised a vast Greek army. Thousands of ships sailed for Troy to reclaim the lovely Helen.

Glossary

mortal a human being, rather than a god or spirit that lives forever

Word cloud

epic **suitors** **jeopardy** **superficial** **renowned**

The Trojan War lasted ten years and many brave heroes died. Eventually, Menelaus challenged Paris to a duel. Paris, whose masculine beauty was greater than his skill with arms, reluctantly agreed. But during their combat, when Paris was at the point of death, Aphrodite whisked him away in a cloud of dust. Helen and Menelaus returned to Sparta and lived happily ever after.

In Homer's **epic** poem *The Iliad*, Helen is blamed for the terrible Trojan War, but by modern standards she may not seem so wicked. Selfish perhaps, but not the **superficial** person she was accused of being. Nevertheless, Helen will always be remembered in Christopher Marlowe's words as having 'the face that launch'd a thousand ships'.

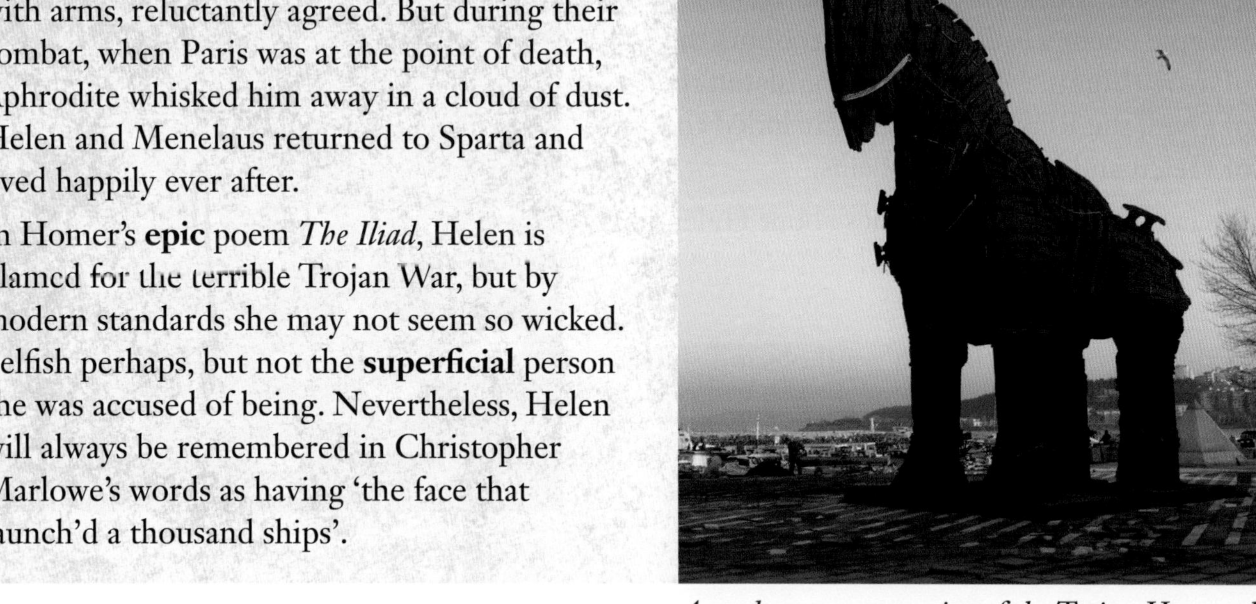

A modern representation of the Trojan Horse, which is the subject of another tale of the Trojan War

Understanding

1. Why did so many chiefs and kings come to Sparta to beg for the hand of Tyndareus' daughter?
2. Who did Helen choose?
3. How did Tyndareus prevent the men Helen rejected from causing trouble?
4. Who were the three goddesses in Troy and what did they want from Paris?
5. Does this story suggest that the idea of beauty was responsible for the Trojan War? Explain your point of view.
6. This is a very ancient story. Think about how it relates to modern times. Can you think of movies, streaming series, songs or shows which have used very similar themes?

Global Perspectives

In a world where information technology brings people closer together, able to communicate in a matter of minutes or even seconds, we might expect problems to be resolved. However, as the story of Helen of Troy shows, a misunderstanding combined with the lack of a swift means of communication can result in devastation. Research some major global situations that could have been avoided. Is avoiding conflict any easier in the modern age?

Word builder

For each of the words in the Word cloud, write a complete sentence in a new context. Try to base your sentences on your examples from question 6 above.

The Trojan War and epic verse

Christopher Marlowe (1564–1593) was an English playwright who read the Greek and Roman classics, part of a normal education at that time. He translated Homer's epic poem *The Iliad*, which recounts the siege of Troy (Ilium). Marlowe also translated the work of Ovid, the Roman poet, who included the story of Helen and Paris in his poems.

Marlowe created these famous lines about Helen of Troy for his play called *Dr Faustus*.

> 'Was this the face that launch'd a thousand ships,
> And burnt the topless towers of Ilium?
>
> (...)
>
> O, thou art fairer than the evening air
> Clad in the beauty of a thousand stars...'

Writing a personal account

Read what happened in the story of Helen of Troy again.

1. Working together, reflect on what the people involved may have thought and felt. Make notes on what made each of them act the way they did. Briefly say what each person did and, in your opinion, why. Be sure to include your observations on:
   - Tyndaraeus
   - Helen
   - Paris
   - Menelaus.
2. Choose one of these characters: Helen, Paris or Menelaus. Look again at what you thought about that person in question 1 above. Consider how this person would speak and what tone of voice they had. Re-tell the story of the Trojan War from that person's point of view.

   Write in the first person (*I*), including:
   - your opinion of the other two people
   - your views on the ten-year war
   - how Helen and Menelaus were reunited.

Developing your language – describing someone's appearance

Use a thesaurus to complete the following tasks.

1. Make a list of at least five words to describe someone with a pleasant appearance.
2. *Handsome* and *good-looking* are adjectives that are often used to describe a boy or man with a pleasant appearance. Find at least two more.
3. *Elegant* and *pretty* are both positive ways to describe a girl or woman.
   - **a** How and why do we use the words *elegant* and *pretty* in different ways?
   - **b** Write a sentence for each word.
4. Look at the words in the box below and decide what they all describe.
   - **a** Put the words into categories. You need to decide what the categories are first.
   - **b** Compare your categories with a partner. If you both have positive and negative categories, do you disagree on any words? If so, why?

crotchety obstinate gregarious surly compassionate
diligent grumpy honourable vengeful argumentative
fussy moody forthright cheerful frank
haughty

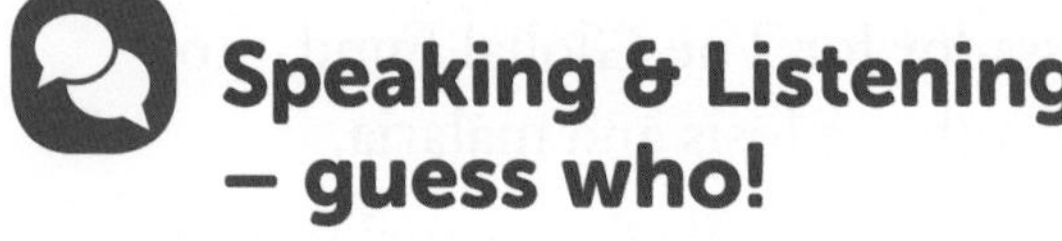

Speaking & Listening – guess who!

Write two or three sentences to describe someone in the classroom but don't say who it is. Read your description aloud and see if the class can guess who it is. Be nice!

Philanthropy profile

In this edition we feature the life and work of Noëlla Coursaris Musunka. Noëlla was born in the Democratic Republic of Congo to a Cypriot father and a Congolese mother. She had a difficult childhood and had to live with relatives, away from her home. Whilst living with relatives she was **allowed** to pursue her education and Noëlla's determination as she progressed through school and then onto higher education led to her **receiving** a degree in Business Management.

Shortly after finishing her degree, Noëlla's friend **entered** her into a modelling competition and she was chosen to appear in a campaign for Agent Provocateur. Noëlla did various campaigns in New York and London and modelling took Noëlla from the pages of fashion magazines like *Vogue*, *Elle* and *Vanity Fair* to a global stage. As she **travelled** the world she always wanted to give back and share her passion for human rights.

At the age of 18, Noëlla returned to her homeland to meet her mother. It was then that the vision for Malaika was **planted** in her heart as she witnessed first-hand the poverty and lack of opportunity for women in the country. In 2007, Noëlla founded Malaika, a non-profit grassroots organisation that empowers Congolese girls and their communities through education and health programmes. Malaika's projects are **impacting** thousands of lives in the community of Kalebuka and in Congo, and are all offered completely free of charge.

These include a school that provides an accredited, holistic curriculum for over 400 girls, a community centre built in partnership with FIFA that provides education, health and sports programmes to over 5,000 youth and adults per year, and clean water for over 30,000 people each year through the building and refurbishment of 21 wells.

Noëlla works to promote and **advocate** the value of education and has reached out beyond the village of Kalebuka to the nation of the Democratic Republic of Congo and the continent of Africa in order to engage with surrounding communities. As one of the leading voices in girls' education in the world, Noëlla is an Ambassador for The Global Fund – to fight Aids, tuberculosis and malaria.

From Noëlla Coursaris' website

Glossary

accredited officially recognised to have met standards by an independent organisation

FIFA football organisation responsible for overseeing the game globally

Understanding

1. Where did Noëlla spend her early childhood?
2. What enabled Noëlla to achieve a Bachelor degree?
3. Why could it be argued that Noëlla took up a career that she was not prepared for?
4. Why do you think Noëlla wanted to give back to the community that she was born into? Analyse the text and find three reasons.
5. In your view, what were the turning points for Noëlla? How much choice would she have had at each of them?
6. In 2017, Noëlla opened a farm at the community centre as part of the Sustainable Pathways project. It forms part of the programme to teach out-of-work youth about conservation farming, entrepreneurship and enterprise development. If Noëlla appointed you as the director of her organisation, what exciting addition to the Malaika community complex would you make?

Word builder

1 All the words in the Word cloud are verbs, but which are in the active form and which are used as passive verbs?

2. Choose three of the words and re-write the sentences in the opposite voice (active or passive) but keeping the context the same. Now evaluate the sentences. Which are more effective?
3. Choose a person who is currently an influencer, perhaps on social media. Write a profile using five of the seven words in the Word cloud. Explore the effectiveness of the verbs by changing the tenses and voices. Feel free to add some of your own verbs.

Word cloud

advocate	**planted**
allowed	**receiving**
entered	**travelled**
impacting	

Global Perspectives

In 2020, the world experienced a global pandemic when the coronavirus Covid-19 spread quickly to almost all countries. Most countries experienced severe damage to their social and economic frameworks. It seemed an ideal opportunity for philanthropy to also spread quickly as so many people were in need of help. Research how your local community responded with philanthropic-style support. During the pandemic, many countries also had an increase in the number of millionaires. How could that happen?

Making adjectives

A *-tic* test

1. Working with a partner, make a list of all the words you know that end in *-tic*, such as *elastic* and *Atlantic*.
2. Divide the words into categories: nouns and adjectives. Some words can be both – look at the examples.

Nouns	Adjectives
elastic	elastic
plastic	plastic

3. Circle all the words you have written down that can be used to describe a person. For example:

realistic

Making adjectives

1. Write down the adjectives for the following nouns:
   - **a** charity
   - **b** philanthropy
   - **c** talent
   - **d** poverty
   - **e** wealth
2. Make verbs from these adjectives:
   - **a** decisive
   - **b** innovative
   - **c** creative
   - **d** critical
   - **e** sympathetic

To test whether you have a verb, make its infinitive with the word *to* ... .

Example: *strong* (adjective) = *to strengthen* (verb)

The order of adjectives in descriptions

When we use two or more adjectives to describe a noun, we often put them in a certain order without thinking about it.

For example, we say:

- a pretty little flowery cup
- an expensive diamond bracelet
- an ugly old wooden chair.

What do you notice about the second word in each of these examples?

We use an *opinion* word before one that is purely descriptive. The object being described comes last.

1. Arrange the following adjectives to describe the objects, then compare with a partner.

Nouns	Adjectives				
A painting	French	priceless	impressionist		
A sports car	new	fantastic	Italian	red	
A band	noisy	amateur	dreadful	Norwegian	rock

The usual order for adjectives is:

opinion → size → shape → age → colour → nationality → material

So you could have:

An elegant, tall, narrow, nineteenth-century, red-roofed, Dutch, brick-built house.

A charming little, star-shaped, ancient, Sri-Lankan silver ring.

2. Working together, write as many adjectives as you can think of in the correct order for the following:

a a well-known monument or castle

b a famous painting or work of art

c a world-famous pop or film star

d a sports car or road-racing bike.

Charisma

Charisma is that special quality that makes somebody appear attractive or makes them influential. A charismatic person can be successful even if they aren't especially talented or good-looking. Listen to three people talking to a TV chat show host about what makes some people popular and influential.

You will hear: Gloria Gift, a pop singer; Mack Malloy, an actor; Stefan Astorius, a concert pianist. Their host is Jo Garcia.

Listen to the audio for this task:

Understanding

1. The guests on the show are all stage performers. What different talents are they famous for?
2. Do they think charisma is more to do with appearance or personality?
3. Do you think Mack's ability as a boy to 'clown about' helped him become successful?
4. Gloria says some backing singers 'don't want the limelight'. In your opinion, what might keep good singers at the back of the stage?
5. Explain in your own words what Stefan means by a 'dangerous aspect of charisma'.
6. Pretend you are the manager of an up and coming social media influencer. They want to increase their popularity, influence and revenue. How would you advise and coach them for success?

Word cloud

aspect
charisma
devious
improvising
influential

Glossary

in the limelight at the front of the stage or the centre of attention. Before electricity, lime (calcium oxide) was heated to light up a stage

Developing your language – figures of speech

Being in the limelight is an expression or a figure of speech. We often use commonly recognised similes and metaphors in informal conversation as a quick way of saying something. Look at what Jo, Mack and Stefan say below and try to find another way to say the words in italics.

1. Jo: *let's get cracking*.
2. Mack: always *showing off* and *cracking jokes*.

3. Jo: You just *bounce onto the stage* and you've got the *audience eating out of your hand*.
4. Stefan: Luck can play a part in getting your first *lucky break*.

Speaking & Listening – talking about charisma

Talk about the following statements. Do you agree or disagree?

1. Charisma is the 'X factor'.
2. All performers – singers, actors and musicians – have got charisma.
3. Some people use their charisma to get what they want.
4. People don't always question why they think someone is wonderful.
5. Charisma is something that can be achieved through practice.
6. It's only charisma that keeps famous performers and actors at the top.

Role-play – an interview

Imagine you are a chat show host. You are going to interview a guest who is well known for using their fame to improve the lives of others.

In pairs, decide who will be the chat show host and who will play the role of the well-known person.

Decide on the following:

- how you will introduce the guest
- how the guest will respond to the introduction
- the area in which the guest would like to improve others' lives
- questions or topics you will exclude from the conversation on this occasion.

Writing a drama script

When you start to write a script, you need to plan the story-line carefully. Then you need to think about your characters. Decide who they are and how they develop and change during the course of the series, or standalone drama. Here are some guidelines to help you write a successful script.

Structure

Most dramas follow the three-act structure.

- **Act One** sets up the challenge your main character has to face. He or she has to encounter an obstacle and overcome it at the end. Remember, the bigger the challenge, the greater the hero.
- In **Act Two**, the character's mission becomes more complicated and the challenge more difficult. Other characters try to prevent or hinder success. Consider introducing a sub-plot. By the end of Act Two, your character is at a low point – about to lose, be eliminated, give up or worse.
- In **Act Three**, your antagonist (villain) reaches a new level of determination and self-awareness. Show them causing more problems, but losing out to the main character, your protaganist. End with a satisfactory 'feel-good' moment.

Remember

A sub-plot is a secondary story, usually introduced early in the second act, and brought to a satisfactory end before the exciting climax to your main story.

Dialogue

Before you start writing dialogue, decide exactly who your characters are. Create mini-biographies for them. Think about: age, education, family background, how they speak and show their emotions. Never write dialogue that doesn't move the story forward, and avoid long speeches. Break up dialogue with action or interjections from other characters. Always read the dialogue aloud to see if it sounds real.

Submitting your proposal

You have been commissioned to write a series which will be shown globally on major streaming channels.

You have been asked to present some ideas to the producers of the series in the form of a proposal. This should include:

- the working title of the series
- the type of drama
- how many episodes are planned and the working titles of each episode
- the main characters
- a synopsis of the plot
- how you will plan for a second series if the first series is a success
- the script for a 3-minute clip to be shown as a 'teaser'.

Before you begin work on your proposal, in small groups discuss some drama series that have featured on streaming channels. What do they have in common? How do they keep the viewers' attention and encourage them to watch subsequent episodes? What makes them a success?

Guess the drama

Here is an excerpt from a teaser for the end of an episode in a series.

1. What type of drama is this?
2. How do you think the next episode would start?

WB

Test the skills you have used in this unit on page 30 of the Workbook.

The Boss:	No, let's just wait and see if they move the merchandise away.
Sergeant:	But we need to get in there now, sir. We have them. We have it all on camera. What more do we need?
The Boss:	I've been in this job for 25 years. Quieten down. They probably know they're being watched. Hold fire until I say the word.

[... after several minutes, the trucks start to leave the compound]

The Boss:	Now. Go. All stations red. Move in. We need to surround them on the exit route, not before.

Establish

After you complete this section, you will be able to:
- ➔ identify the key components of a good summary
- ➔ focus on appropriate content and suitable language
- ➔ write a synopsis based on a range of input material.

Read the article below, which is the first part of an extended summary of the arrest of one of the most influential criminals in British history. As you read, think about the following points, without writing anything down.

- What the extract is summarising (the content)
- Specified details (the theme that holds the piece together)
- How the writing is structured (to suit its purpose and audience)
- Choice of language

Tip

Although a synopsis can be thought of as a type of summary, it is a survey and is usually shorter and broader in scope than a summary. Summaries are usually more detailed and cover specified areas.

Account of the arrest of Dr Crippen

The *Montrose* was in port at Antwerp when I read in the *Continental Daily Mail* that a warrant had been issued for Crippen and le Neve. They were reported to have been traced to a hotel in Brussels but had then vanished again.

S.S. "MONTROSE"

Soon after we sailed to Quebec I happened to glance through the porthole of my cabin and behind a lifeboat I saw two men. One was squeezing the other's hand. I walked along the boat deck and got into a conversation with the elder man. I noticed that there was a mark on the bridge of his nose through wearing spectacles, that he had recently shaved off a moustache, and that he was growing a beard. The young fellow was very reserved, and I remarked about his cough.

"Yes", said the elder man, "my boy has a weak chest, and I'm taking him to California for his health."

I retuned to my cabin and had another look at the *Daily Mail*. I studied the description and photographs issued by Scotland

Yard. Crippen was 50 years of age, 5 ft 4 inches high, wearing spectacles and a moustache; Miss Le Neve was 27, 5 ft 5 inches, slim, with pale complexion. I then examined the passenger list and ascertained that the two passengers were travelling as 'Mr Robinson and son'. I arranged for them to take meals at my table.

When the bell went for lunch, I tarried until the coast was clear, then slipped into the Robinsons' cabin unobserved, where I noticed two things: that the boy's felt hat was packed around the rim to make it fit, and that he had been using a piece of a woman's bodice as a face flannel. That satisfied me. I went down to the dining saloon and kept my eyes open. The boy's manners at table were ladylike. Later, when they were promenading the saloon deck, I went out and walked behind them, and called out, "Mr Robinson!" I had to shout the name several times before the man turned and said to me, "I'm sorry, Captain, I didn't hear you – this cold wind is making me deaf."

In the next two days we developed our acquaintance. Mr Robinson was the acme of politeness, quiet-mannered, a non-smoker; at night he went on deck and roamed about on his own. Once the wind blew up his coat tails and in his hip pocket I saw a revolver. After that I also carried a revolver, and we often had pleasant little tea parties in my cabin, discussing the book he was reading, which was *The Four Just Men*, a murder mystery by Edgar Wallace – and when that little fact was wirelessed to London and published it made Edgar Wallace's name ring, so agog was everybody in England over the Crippen case.

That brings me to the wireless. On the third day out I gave my wireless operator a message for Liverpool: *One hundred and thirty miles west of Lizard… have strong suspicions that Crippen London cellar murderer and accomplice are among saloon passengers… accomplice dressed as a boy; voice, manner and build undoubtedly a girl.*

I remember Mr Robinson sitting in a deckchair, looking at the wireless aerials and listening to the crackling of our crude spark-transmitter, and remarking to me what a wonderful invention it was.

Tip

An account is likely to be a summary for these reasons: it will start at the beginning, contain a middle section with specified and relevant details, and it will provide an ending which satisfies the reader. An account is also likely be chronological, whereas most summaries are not.

Engage

Now engage with the text more closely to answer the following ten questions.

1. What can you infer from the opening sentence?
2. When did you realise that the narrator, using the first person, was the captain?
3. Where in the extract is the first instance of very specific detail? What did you think?
4. A lot more detail is given in this sentence:

   'I then examined the passenger list and ascertained that the two passengers were travelling as 'Mr Robinson and son'.'

   Why has the writer chosen to use inverted commas around 'Mr Robinson and son'?
5. In the line, 'I tarried until the coast was clear, then slipped into the Robinsons cabin unobserved …', there is a shift in the use of language. How does the language change?
6. Three words are used to convey the captain's suspicions. What are they?
7. What does the use of the words and phrases 'promenading' (line 29), 'was the acme of politeness' (line 35), 'agog' (line 43) and 'wireless' (line 50) suggest?
8. 'After that I carried a revolver, and we often had pleasant little tea parties together in my cabin.' What does this sentence tell you about the two characters?
9. Towards the end of the extract, the captain sends a synopsis to the port of Liverpool. Is it accurate? How could you improve it to attract the attention of the authorities?
10. What is the irony in the final words of the final paragraph?

Tip

It's always a good idea to scan an extract before you read it thoroughly. Use your pre-reading skills and try to get the gist of the piece as early as possible. Context clues will help with unfamiliar words, and establishing the purpose and audience will help. When you have a good sense of what is going on, your understanding and appreciation will increase.

Writing a synopsis

Now have a go at writing a synopsis. You are Dr Crippen's accomplice, Miss Le Neve, and very early on you suspect that the captain is on to you. You have another accomplice who is also onboard ship.

1. Send a telegraph message in a similar style to the captain's message to Liverpool. You can think of this as an antique version of a Tweet.
2. Using the first person and imitating the style and language of the extract, create a synopsis of your plan so that your accomplice can 'save your day'.

Writing a summary

You may know how this story ends. However, be creative and invent a different chain of events that occur after Dr Crippen was sitting in his deckchair and remarking on the wonders of radio. Change the narrative voice to the third person and write a summary of what happens for the rest of the voyage and when the ship docks. As this is a summary, you will need to incorporate specific details, suitable sequencing and a concise conclusion. Dr Crippen does not necessarily need to be caught.

Think about what you have learned about the key components of a summary and a synopsis. The differences are subtle. Now explore this further by evaluating three attempts at a synopsis of the full account of Dr Crippen's voyage and subsequent arrest.

To make it interesting, the writers come from different contexts and therefore use different approaches and styles. However, their aim is the same – to provide the key details and to keep it short whilst creating maximum impact for the reader or listener.

1. As you read each synopsis, think about the context. Who is speaking? What is their angle on the account?
2. Which synopsis do you think is strongest? Which is satisfactory? Which one needs some tidying up? Give reasons for your judgment.

The end of Dr Crippen

Dr Crippen got arrested by the policeman who was waiting for him at the port of Quebec. That was it. All over for one of the most influential criminals of the Victorian age in London, England. The police were happy. They got their man. And they also got their woman, Miss Le Neve, as she was with Dr Crippen at the time. It started on the boat in England when the two criminals tried to escape – and it ended when it all ended in cuffs.

In another story, we can report that Tigress, the cat who has been missing for a week, has been found and she is doing really well.

What really happened on the *Montrose*

From the outset, Captain Kendall had his suspicions. After reading in a national newspaper that Dr Crippen was on the run with his female accomplice, and that they had evaded the authorities in London, the captain was sure that they would not evade the security of the *Montrose*. Not under his command.

As soon as Captain Kendall observed the lack of spectacles, the recently removed moustache and the new growth of a beard, he had his man. All that remained was to entice Crippen into the open and secure further evidence. The sight of a hidden revolver further inspired Kendall to act quickly but quietly. Little did he know that a pot of tea and a wireless radio would do the trick. Crippen and Le Neve were calmly cajoled into a comfort zone that would provide the basis for the arrest. It was an anxious night but on arrival at Quebec, Inspector Dew, surprised the famous passengers and introduced himself with a pair of shiny handcuffs.

A good job done by all

I would like to convey my heartfelt thanks to the whole team for their work on this difficult and influential case. As you know, we have spent months tracking down Dr Crippen and his accomplice, and we nearly had them in Brussels, but they slipped away again. Thanks to a very astute Captain Kendall on board the *Montrose*, we were tipped off in good time to get our Inspector and some officers to Canada to make the arrest. Let me say here that we do not encourage the general public to take matters of catching criminals into their own hands. Please do your best to stand back and report concerns to the local police. Captain Kendall is different as he is trained in combat and licensed to carry a firearm.

Enable

At the beginning of this Assessment workshop, one of your targets was to write a good synopsis, using the key components you would expect to see in a summary and tailoring the synopsis to suit the specific angle required.

You have just examined the strengths and weaknesses of three synopses. Now it's your turn to put what you have learned into practice.

Consider the different types of source material on the next page.

… and, after a 15-year absence, this is still the most influential pairing of like-minded people that ever lived. They left us at the end of the last series at the height of anticipation, but a follow-up just didn't happen. Not until now that is. In the first episode, we see …

Saw the first episode last night. Those two have not lost their charm. On the edge of my seat and can't wait for next week. Talk about tension.

Interviewer: You're known as the 'Influencer of Hollywood' – anything that moves and shakes in Tinseltown is usually connected to you. Can I ask why you think this series and this location has worked so well?

Director: You're very kind, and yes, I have been directing feature movies, mainly, for the last 25 years. I wanted a change of focus, a change of genre. And we chose the location first actually. It's such a unique place and it sets a fantastic scene for the series. Captures the mood beautifully.

Never has the sight of two old friends meeting up again been more comforting

Yes, I did wonder if the excitement and relevance of the first series would still be there. We are living in a very different time, of course, post-pandemic and looking to a brighter future. I was honoured to have been invited to write the second series, but I did approach it differently. This series is thinner, stripped-down, targeted – and the better for it. But I'd better not give too much away!

Follow up – writing a synopsis

Respond to the task below.

Write a synopsis based on the context and clues in the source material. You can choose the heading, style, narrative voice, language and specific detail. You will need to embellish the existing content and you are allowed some creativity. Your aim is to attract the reader or listener.

The word count is up to you but be sure that your synopsis is neither too long nor too short. Once you have conveyed your message with an appropriate amount of detail, you should feel confident that you have the right number of words.

When you have finished, discuss your synopsis with your teacher.

Tip

An important skill for success in English exams and tests is the ability to draw upon a range of source material with a common theme in order to collate the information and present it in a different format. For example, you may be asked to read two extracts with similar themes and to choose elements from both for a new purpose.

4 The impact of tourism

In this unit, you will engage with the impact of travel and tourism in some extreme and unusual places. You will read about a tropical paradise in the Orinoco Delta, discover what it is really like to encounter a moose, listen to a customer's telephone complaint and present your own arguments about your dream destination. You will also write a travel blog of your own, based on careful research and using a lively and persuasive style.

And in doing all that, you will be practising these key skills:

Speaking & Listening

- Adapt your talk in the context of the tourist industry for maximum impact, whether speaking persuasively or to complain.
- Evaluate the effectiveness of your own talk and that of others about dream destinations, and give feedback about persuasion.

Writing

- Make careful choices of adjectives and language techniques to give information about the impact of exotic places on people.
- Combine linguistic and structural choices in order to write persuasively about destinations, with convincing use of detail.

Reading

- Analyse the use of imagery by travel writers for different effects.
- Explore how formal and informal writing conveys writers' feelings about unusual places and creatures.

Assessment workshop

You will gain practice in the key assessment skill of responding to multiple-choice short-answer comprehension questions on non-fiction texts. You will identify different types of answers and the skills they test, then practise writing your own multiple-choice questions.

Thinking time

The number of people who flew on scheduled airline flights in 2019 was over 4.5 billion, but that number was halved by the global pandemic in 2020 and 2021. What do you think will be the future of travel and tourism? Will we make fewer but more memorable journeys?

1. How many of the iconic structures in the composite picture on the opposite page can you name?
2. What kind of company would use an a picture like that to promote its business?
3. What do you think the top quotation means?
4. Do you think the journey or the destination is the most important part of travelling?
5. As we travel, how can we visit different places safely without risking ourselves or damaging nature and the environment?

"A journey of a thousand miles must begin with a single step."
Lao Tzu

"The world is a book and those who do not travel read only one page."
St Augustine

"One's destination is never a place, but a new way of seeing things."
Henry Miller

Speaking & Listening – dream destination game

The object of the game is to persuade your fellow group members to agree with your choice of destination.

1. Each member of the group writes down the name of a place they would love to visit one day and five reasons for their choice.
2. Taking it in turns, each member presents their argument by describing their dream destination and explaining why they have chosen it above all others.
3. While this is happening, the other members of the group assess the performance by giving it marks out of five in each of these categories:
   - **a** Does the destination sound appealing?
   - **b** Would you like to go there?
   - **c** How persuasive is the argument presented?
4. The winner is the one who gains the highest mark out of 15 once all the group members have presented.

Paradise in Los Roques

Los Roques is a coral archipelago 150 km off the coast of Venezuela consisting of 42 small islands surrounding a huge lagoon. Here, in this **paradisiacal** playground, hurricanes hardly happen. The days are hot and the nights are cool. Venezuelans visit at weekends to snorkel, scuba dive and watch the sunset, returning to Gran Roque, the only **inhabited** island, for dinner and a **comfortable** night in one of the many **delightful** *posadas*.

Following in the wake of Christopher Columbus and Walter Raleigh, we took a boat up the Orinoco River. Our guides encouraged us to take a dip in the river at sunset. It looked **inviting** – the wide dark waters tinged with pink, parrots winging their way home above a wall of green jungle. A young Belgian couple took the plunge. But are there crocodiles? And piranha fish? Yes! But there are also electric-blue morph butterflies with wings as large as your hand, noisy families of red howler monkeys and the part-reptile guacharaca bird, a hang-over from pre-historic times.

There was also plenty of wildlife activity at the jungle camp. A **magnificent** puma, brought in as a baby by the Indians, paced the length of its enclosure. In the rafters of the dining room an ocelot and a racoon played together while a family of otters honked noisily for scraps at our table. A huge tarantula sitting on an **adjacent** banana plant caused a stir. The young Belgian took it on the back of his hand but his mosquito repellent irritated the spider which slowly 'hunched up', a sign that it was ready to deliver its poison. Our guide gently coaxed it back to its leaf – no harm done!

The Orinoco Delta is home to the Warao Indians. The river is their highway and the canoe their only mode of transport. (...) The Warao believe they came from the stars and their god brought them to the Orinoco Delta, to paradise, where the Mareche, the 'tree of life', grows in abundance. The Mareche produces an orange fruit which, when softened for several days, makes a **palatable** juice (...). The young tree yields a string from which hammocks and baskets are made. When the tree rots it is home to a large, yellow grub, an excellent source of protein – eaten live. I was offered a chance to try this wriggling delicacy – I just wasn't hungry!

From 'Children of the Stars' by Angela Clarence, *The Observer* (5 November 2000)

Word cloud

adjacent	**inviting**
comfortable	**magnificent**
delightful	**palatable**
inhabited	**paradisiacal**

Understanding

1. According to Angela Clarence, what is it about the Los Roques islands which make them like paradise?
2. What are the risks of taking a swim in the Orinoco River at sunset?
3. Why do tourists nevertheless take those risks?
4. What examples does Angela Clarence use to suggest this is a place where wildlife behaves as if it is tame?
5. How far does the writing convince you that the Orinoco Delta really is a kind of paradise? Select details from the text to support your answer.
6. Write your own description of what a natural paradise would be like, in which human beings allow nature to thrive without trying to tame it.

Glossary

coral archipelago a group of small islands surrounded by a coral reef

guacharaca bird also called a *chalaca* or *cocorico*, these ancient birds look a bit like turkeys and are only found in Venezuela, Colombia and Tobago

ocelot a wild cat native to the Americas

posadas (*Spanish*) inns or hostels

tarantula a large and often hairy spider

Global Perspectives

The world has become a smaller place and it is much easier to visit exotic and unusual destinations. Evaluate the advantages and disadvantages of continuing to develop a region's infrastructure to meet the needs of an influx of tourists. Do the benefits of any improvements justify the risks to the natural environment of the local area? Is so-called eco-tourism the way to go now?

Word builder

In 'Children of the Stars', the writer suggests that the people of the Orinoco Delta live in a kind of ideal innocent relationship with nature. However, she first sets the scene by describing the islands and the lagoon, which are much more what you might expect in a holiday paradise, before exploring further.

The words in the Word cloud are carefully chosen adjectives to make the bridge between an ordinary holiday and an extraordinary travel adventure. They establish the mood and prepare us for the idea of an earthly paradise.

1. Which of the definitions for each word below best fits the tone the writer wants to establish? The first is completed for you as an example.

   a paradisiacal = busy and buzzing / perfect and unspoilt / modern and new

   'perfect and unspoilt' because 'paradisiacal' creates the impression that this is an unspoilt part of the world in a perfect relationship with nature

   b inhabited = populated and civilised / lonely and abandoned / untouched and wild

   c comfortable = cramped and noisy / strange and unsettling / calm and cosy

   d delightful = attractive and homely / sophisticated and chic / outdated and shabby

   e inviting = welcoming and tempting / cold and clammy / harsh and hostile

   f magnificent = repelling and strange / wild and dangerous / impressive and powerful

   g adjacent = remote and spiky / close and convenient / dangerous and poisonous

   h palatable = inedible and nasty / bitter and sharp / drinkable and delicious

2. Use one adjective to set the mood for each of these travel destinations:

   a a rundown old hotel

   b a theme park

   c a botanical garden.

Using adjectives for effect

Carefully chosen adjectives can help the writer to create the atmosphere within a piece of writing.

1. Read the following passage:

   The cavernous room dwarfed the terrified rescuer. Unused as he was to the echoing chamber of the supposedly deserted building, each clattering footstep and skittering rat filled his heart with dread forebodings of his imminent destruction. With his hands shaking with uncontrolled fear, his brow sweating profusely and his teeth chattering in the intense cold, he reluctantly continued on his fruitless search.

2. The adjectives used in this passage raise a lot of questions for the reader. For example, the use of *cavernous* to describe the size of the room suggests it is very big, so the questions that arise are:

   Why is it such a big room?

   What kind of room is it?

   What is its purpose?

   a Make a list of the other adjectives in the passage.

   b Draw four text boxes (or bubbles) and place one of the adjectives in each. Fill the remaining space in each box (bubble) with the questions the reader would want answers to.

   c Choose three of your own adjectives to describe the overall atmosphere created in the passage.

3. Now it is your turn. Write a short paragraph in the style of the one above where your use of adjectives creates questions in the mind of the reader.

Remember

The use of carefully chosen adjectives combined with well-chosen facts and details can engage the reader in non-narrative writing. The opening paragraph of 'Children of the Stars' is an effective example of this technique.

Our friend the moose

Bill Bryson relates the 'sad' case of the endangered moose in North America.

Goodness knows why anyone would want to shoot an animal as harmless and **retiring** as the moose, but thousands do – so many, in fact, that states now hold lotteries to decide who gets a licence. (...)

Hunters will tell you that a moose is a wily and ferocious forest creature. In fact, a moose is a cow drawn by a three-year-old. That's all there is to it. Without doubt, the moose is the most **improbable**, endearingly hopeless creature ever to live in the wilds. It is huge – as big as a horse – but magnificently **ungainly**. A moose runs as if its legs have never been introduced to each other. Even its antlers are hopeless. Other creatures grow antlers with sharp points that look wonderful in profile and command the respect of adversaries. Moose grow antlers that look like oven gloves.

Above all what distinguishes the moose is its almost **boundless** lack of intelligence. If you are driving down a highway and a moose steps from the woods ahead of you, he will squint at you for a long minute, then abruptly hie off down the road away from you, legs flailing in eight directions at once. Never mind that there are perhaps 10,000 square miles of safe, dense forest on either side of the highway. **Clueless** as to where he is and what exactly is going on, the moose doggedly follows the highway (...) before his peculiar gait inadvertently steers him back into the woods, where he immediately stops and takes on a **perplexed** expression that says, 'Hey – woods. Now how (...) did I get here?'

From *Notes From A Big Country* by Bill Bryson

Word cloud

boundless
clueless
improbable
perplexed
retiring
ungainly

Glossary

lotteries state-held raffles

drawn by a three-year-old badly drawn

endearingly hopeless lovable but without hope

legs flailing in eight directions with an uncontrolled running action

doggedly follows the highway stubbornly moves along the road

Understanding

1. What kind of landscape does the moose live in?
2. How do we know that moose-hunting is very popular?
3. What is the writer's opinion of the moose's looks?
4. How does the writer illustrate the clumsiness of the moose?
5. How do his opinions contrast with those of hunters?
6. What does Bryson's use of humour encourage you to think about moose-hunting?

Developing your language – creating an image

A successful writer will use a series of ideas to build an image for the reader. One of the ways Bill Bryson builds his image of the moose as a charming but stupid animal is by using humour to make the creature seem comical. For example:

- 'a moose is a cow drawn by a three-year-old' – the image makes the shape of the animal seem simple and childish
- 'A moose runs as if its legs have never been introduced to each other.' – makes the moose seem uncoordinated and clumsy
- 'he will squint at you for a long minute' – makes the moose sound dim-witted because it takes a long time to understand what is happening.

What image does each of these statements suggest?

a 'legs flailing in eight directions at once'

b 'Moose grow antlers that look like oven gloves.'

c 'his peculiar gait inadvertently steers him back into the woods'

d 'Hey – woods. Now how (...) did I get here?'

Word builder

Look at the six adjectives listed in the Word cloud. They are all used to describe the moose in a way that is uncomplimentary and comical.

Match each adjective from the Word cloud to the correct explanation of the effect to build a more detailed and unflattering image of the moose as interpreted by the writer.

boundless	it is shy and avoids human contact
clueless	its lack of intelligence has no limits
improbable	it is easily confused
perplexed	it is clumsy and uncoordinated
retiring	it is difficult to believe an animal like this exists
ungainly	it has no idea what it is doing

Global Perspectives

Sadly, there has been a global increase in what could be called 'hunting tourism', or the desire to visit a country to exploit its indigenous animals and wildlife. This industry has many facets from illegal activities to legal but unsavoury and immoral behaviour. Evaluate this trend, noting some potential reasons for its growth.

Using juxtaposition

A juxtaposition is when two ideas or concepts are placed next to each other to create a contrast or comparison.

Bill Bryson creates his comical image of the moose using a series of images that are juxtaposed. For example:

'Hunters will tell you that a moose is a wily and ferocious forest creature. In fact, a moose is a cow drawn by a three-year-old.'

1. Copy and complete the following table to map the use of juxtaposition.

What the hunters claim	Meaning	How the writer interprets it	Meaning
wily and ferocious		a cow drawn by a three-year-old	Passive and too comical to be dangerous
it is huge – as big as a horse	It is powerful and graceful	but magnificently ungainly	
other creatures grow antlers with sharp points			They look soft and fluffy and completely harmless

2. Now it is time for you to create your own juxtaposition. Choose an animal from the list below:

Ostrich	Polar bear	Giraffe	Panda	Koala
Chicken	Sheep	Sloth	Porcupine	Orang-utan

a Make a list of the main features of your chosen animal, both in terms of its physical appearance and personality.

b You are aiming for a comic image so write down an alternative interpretation for each feature in your list.

c Once you are satisfied, write a blog entry about meeting your chosen animal.

d Use your blog entry to play the 30 seconds game. The aim of the game is to read out your description without mentioning what animal you've chosen. Your audience must try to guess the name of the animal within 30 seconds of you starting your description.

Using oxymorons

An oxymoron is a specific kind of juxtaposition, being a combination of words that appear to contradict each other but, when used together, create an image offering a different meaning.

Bill Bryson uses an oxymoron to create contrast as the moose is described as 'endearingly hopeless'.

He uses 'endearingly' to suggest the moose is an animal that people feel affection for but he contrasts this with the idea of it being 'hopeless', suggesting how pathetic it is.

Normally, you wouldn't be so fond of something that is so useless but Bryson suggests this is one of the reasons why a moose is so likeable.

1. Another oxymoron used is 'magnificently ungainly'.

   Explain the meaning of this phrase and how it works as an oxymoron.

2. Using oxymorons is common among writers. Here are three examples from Shakespeare:

   a 'O brawling love!'

   b 'O loving hate!'

   c 'Sweet sorrow'

   Explain why each of these is an oxymoron. (Hint: *brawling* is another word for fighting.)

3. Here are some more examples of oxymorons. What effect does each one create?

   a bitter-sweet

   b hot ice

   c thunderous silence

   d random order

   e wise fool

   f original copy

4. You can make up some of your own oxymorons. Aim for at least three.

   Just think of an emotion and add an opposite to it, e.g. clearly confused.

Remember

Oxymoron is from two Greek words meaning sharp and dull, which is itself an example of an oxymoron.

Courtesy call

Listen to the audio for this task:

Word cloud

aeon
dishevelled
eternity
mortified
penitentiary

Understanding

Courtesy calls are usually made in order to gauge customer satisfaction, with little expectation that there will be a problem.

1. What is the name of the travel company?
2. Why might Ling have been unsettled by the way the conversation developed?
3. What is your impression of the customer from the way she responds during the call?
4. Does the customer's use of exaggeration support her grievances or detract from them?
5. How might the travel agency representative have handled the call differently and would it have been appropriate to do so?
6. In pairs, role-play making a complaint to a hotel receptionist about your hotel room. Your partner will deal politely with your complaint.

Glossary

courtesy call a phone call by a company to check a service has been provided appropriately

family solicitor lawyer representing a family

Formula 1 high-speed racing category

haul (your company) over the coals severely scold (your company) (an idiomatic expression)

taste buds a group of cells on the tongue and in the mouth that identify taste

Word builder

Hyperbole uses exaggeration to emphasise a point. Each word in the Word cloud is an example of hyperbole.

When she claims that the eight-hour flight took an 'aeon' to complete, the customer doesn't really mean it lasted for an indefinite amount of time but that it seemed to last forever.

1. How are 'aeon' and 'eternity' similar in the effect their usage creates?

2. When she claims the driver looked 'dishevelled' what does she really mean?
3. What image does the use of 'Formula 1 driver' suggest when she describes the driver's performance?
4. What do you think the customer means by 'mortified'?

   rigid with fear / embarrassed and humiliated / feeling sick
5. What does describing a hotel as a 'penitentiary' suggest about its treatment of guests?
6. Does the use of hyperbole paint an effective picture of how terrible the holiday was or does it say more about the customer's attitude?

Developing your language – using modal verbs

Modal verbs can be used to indicate if something is possible, probable or certain. They can also be used to make requests and give permission.

The most common modal verbs are:

can could may might shall should will would

In 'Courtesy call' the travel agent begins with a polite request:

'Might I take a few moments of your time?'

The customer replies with a statement of permission:

'You may take some of my valuable time.'

Can you recognise the modal verb in each of the sentences below and say what function it is serving?

Functions: possible probable certain request suggestion

1. Could it have been any worse, I ask myself?
2. I would like to say it was, but I am afraid I can't.
3. I should warn you...
4. Can we start at the beginning, please?
5. Well, we will definitely investigate what happened.
6. Shall I take you through meal after meal to prove my point?
7. I can assure you that we, as a company, will investigate this matter.

Writing a travel blog

You are going to write a travel blog about a place that has been impacted by tourism. It could be a place you have been to or one that you have researched. It is likely to be a beautiful place that appreciates visitors, such as Morocco, as described below. However, there will also be another dimension to the place which makes it special even when tourists are not there.

This extract from a travel blog about Morocco describes a Sunday morning in a village in Ait Bougmez valley.

The silence was deafening as I sipped cafe au lait overlooking the peaceful village and the valley below. Men worked the small plots of land by hand, using what seemed to be ancient tools. But they have an important role as the food produced would nourish the family throughout the summer months and provide a stock for the winter months. The apple and peach trees provided a pop of colour in the already green landscape with the snow-capped Atlas Mountains towering around. Children wandered freely through the village, playing with what little toys they had while the women sat chatting amongst each other. Meanwhile donkeys were led through the village en route to work.

From *Why Morocco?* by Mandy Sinclair

Speaking & Listening – the destination game

Find out how much you know about the destination you have chosen to write your blog about.

Write questions on ten cue cards, e.g. What is the best feature / the most important building / the attitude of the locals / the thing you like doing most / the best time to visit / the most unusual local custom?

In pairs, shuffle the cards, then take turns to pick one and ask the question written on it. The other player has 20 seconds to answer.

Writing frame for a travel blog

Use the guidelines below to plan and draft your travel blog.

Remember that you are writing as if you are in the place being described and that you have a key message to send to your reader, so the more convincing you are, the better your blog will be received.

Key features of a travel blog

- Non-fiction text
- Personal experiences
- Sends a deeper message
- Retains a colourful and exciting mood to ensure balance

WB Test the skills you have used in this unit on page 39 of the Workbook.

Do your research

- Find out about your chosen destination.
- Make a note of some interesting facts and statistics to use in your blog. Both help to convince an audience you know what you are writing about.
- Collect some images you can use to highlight the points you make.

  Remember that a picture really does paint a thousand words!

Plan carefully

- Decide what details you want to include about your destination – don't try to cram too much in.
- It is better to highlight a few carefully chosen features than try to cover everything.
- Before beginning your blog, decide on the order of the paragraphs and where you are going to use your images.

Narrative style

- A blog is personal so write in the first person narrative.
- Keep it fairly informal to create the bond between you and your audience.
- Adopt a lively, fast-paced style to help persuade the audience they are sharing the experience.

It's all in the detail

- You are the audience's eyes. They see everything through your description so make your details count.
- Use reflection to allow your audience to share your feelings about your experience.
- Write about the people as well as the place to add another dimension that offers an alternative view of some of the impacts of tourism.

Establish

After you complete this section, you will be able to:

- ➔ recognise some of the literary and language features used in non-fiction writing
- ➔ appreciate the structural features of informative and persuasive texts
- ➔ develop your understanding of short answer multiple-choice questions (MCQs) by constructing some of your own.

First, read this text inviting you to visit Venice.

Tip

The text below is primarily an information text with persuasive features. In tests you will see both information and persuasive texts. Assessment of non-fiction texts tests your understanding of implicit and explicit facts, and how writers use language and structure to persuade you to share their viewpoint. Some of the questions will be multiple-choice.

Historic Venice

Mists and masked balls in palace and piazza, romance, pageant and splendour. Take a step out of reality and enjoy five unforgettable days in romantic, historic Venice.

Perhaps you think you know it already. You've seen the Bond movies, the ads featuring gondoliers steering enraptured tourists through the Grand Canal. But Venice is far more than picturesque bridges. Come and discover its hidden corners. Take a turn through historic streets, see its architecture and experience its other-worldly atmosphere. Wander the City of Water with a loved one or join a group walk with an experienced guide, who'll tell you about Canaletto and the peccadilloes of the wicked Lord Byron.

Stop to listen to a string quartet, drink the best espresso as you wait for your vaporetto, take a trip to Murano or wander through colourful street markets. And then, when you've found the real Venice, see the Bridge of Sighs, the Doge's Palace, the Piazza San Marco and the Rialto Bridge.

Once a powerful state, home to bankers and speculators, Venice is now a UNESCO World Heritage Site and the most delightful car-free zone in Europe. But Venice is under threat from rising water levels. Be sure to see this enchanting City of Light, before it's too late!

Engage

Below are some typical multiple-choice questions that you might see in an exam. Think about the question types and then consider the range of answers that follow.

Work in pairs. While you are answering the questions on the passage about Venice, discuss the objective and structure of each question. Engage with the question types – don't just answer them.

1. What literary technique does the writer use in the first sentence? Tick (✓) **one** box.

   Metaphor ☐
   Alliteration ☐
   Onomatopoeia ☐

2. Identify **one** word from the second paragraph which means 'like a picture'. Tick (✓) **one** box.

   'enraptured' ☐
   'peccadilloes' ☐
   'picturesque' ☐

3. Give **two** reasons, according to the writer, that people all over the world think they know about Venice. Tick (✓) **one** box.

   They have researched travel brochures and the internet. ☐
   They have learned from geography and history lessons. ☐
   They have seen James Bond films and advertisements with gondoliers. ☐

4. 'Come', 'Take', 'Wander'. These verbs begin each sentence at the beginning of the second paragraph. What kind of verb are they? Tick (✓) **one** box.

   Imperatives ☐
   Conditionals ☐
   Participles ☐

5. Identify **two** reasons the writer gives to suggest why you should visit Venice's 'hidden corners' before visiting the famous sites. Tick (✓) **one** box.
   - The main sights are always very busy and there are long queues. ☐
   - You should learn something and soak up the atmosphere first. ☐
   - You should get used to travelling by water and do some shopping first. ☐
6. In the final paragraph, the writer implies that Venice may not survive for long. Why? Tick (✓) **one** box.
   - Because of climate change, water levels are rising, so the city will soon be under water and lost. ☐
   - Soon, nobody will want to live in a car-free city any more. ☐
   - The buildings are very old and falling down. ☐
7. Give **two** structural features of an information text which can be found in the passage. Tick (✓) **one** box.
   - The text is written in the third person and uses scientific vocabulary. ☐
   - The text uses a formal style and topic sentences. ☐
   - The text uses lists and instructs the reader through imperatives. ☐

Did you choose the best multiple-choice answers? Did you come across any distractors (an answer that could be seen to be correct but actually isn't)?

Tip

Questions are set to align to the flow and order of the text but they get progressively more difficult. They start with what is explicit and move to what is implicit. They start by asking you to find aspects of language and vocabulary, and then to make inferences based on the information in the text.

Evaluate

It is important to recognise what each question is attempting to test, as this can guide you towards the best answer. Here are the question types associated with each of the seven questions in the Engage section.

1. **Literary techniques question**

   The distractors are all other literary techniques, so you need to revise literary techniques for non-fiction texts as well as fiction.

2. **Vocabulary question**

   You need to find an adjective and ensure it fits the question. Think about word stems, parts of speech and meaning.

3. **Understanding question**

   You need to look at what the writer says explicitly here. Don't make guesses of your own.

4. **Grammar question**

   In this case, imperatives encourage the reader to see the unusual sights of Venice.

5. **Understanding question**

   This question tests implicit understanding. You can work out what is implied from the suggestion that you should 'find the real Venice' before visiting the sites. You are asked for your own words, not words from the passage. The distractors may be true but they are not implied by information in the text.

6. **Understanding question**

   This tests your understanding of the relationship between explicit and implied information. You are told 'water levels are rising', so what does this imply?

7. **Structure question**

   All three answers give features of information texts but only the third one is a response to this information text. Can you also identify the features of a persuasive text?

Tip

Be sure you can recognise the different structural features of information and persuasive texts. Information texts are usually in the third person, communicate facts in an organised and sequenced way, and explain the facts. Persuasive texts use language for particular effects on the reader.

Work in groups of three. Your task is to:

1. Choose a short information text of about 100 words.
2. Select the question type you want to test.
3. Think of three possible answers:
   - one that is correct and precise
   - one that is a really good distractor
   - one that is wrong but tempting nonetheless.
4. Now pass your text and question to another group, while you receive theirs. Identify their question type, choose the correct answer and note how effective their distractor is.
5. With the other group evaluate the mulitple-choice questions.

Enable

At the beginning of this Assessment workshop, one of your targets was to understand how different question types test different skills. You are going to construct your own multiple-choice questions.

First, read this informative and persuasive text.

Antarctica expedition

How about a unique and exciting trip to Antarctica this summer? You can frolic to its fantastically frosted vistas. You may have thought that this most southerly destination is beyond reach for a vacation. However, its untarnished areas can remain so but with your presence. Antarctica is still a challenge and is reachable only by navigators with specialist knowledge and training.

In the early days of exploration, scrupulous planning was required to ensure safety and success. Today, small groups on specially designed boats can go where previous explorers ventured and enjoy the sights they saw. Tourists just have to agree to some strict guidelines. Icebergs like mountains, glaciers melting away in skyscraper-chunks and clear blue skies create mesmerising views.

In the winter, the nearly constant dark can be dismal. It's a desolate scene and much of life is on hold. In the endless daylight of the summer, however, you will see penguins, albatross and free-roaming mighty whales. Your route will take you past the breeding grounds of thousands of seals, which sunbathe without a care on sheets of floating ice, sliding around with the ease of an Olympic ice dancer.

There are options: travel to Vostok Station near the South Pole; transfer to West Antarctica and see the Transantarctic Mountain range; head off via the Antarctic Circle to journey to Argentina. If you stay in the Circle you will see that wildlife is cared for much like the Crown Jewels of England. Once you get home, you will surely appreciate that you reclined the offer of a ticket on a cruise liner.

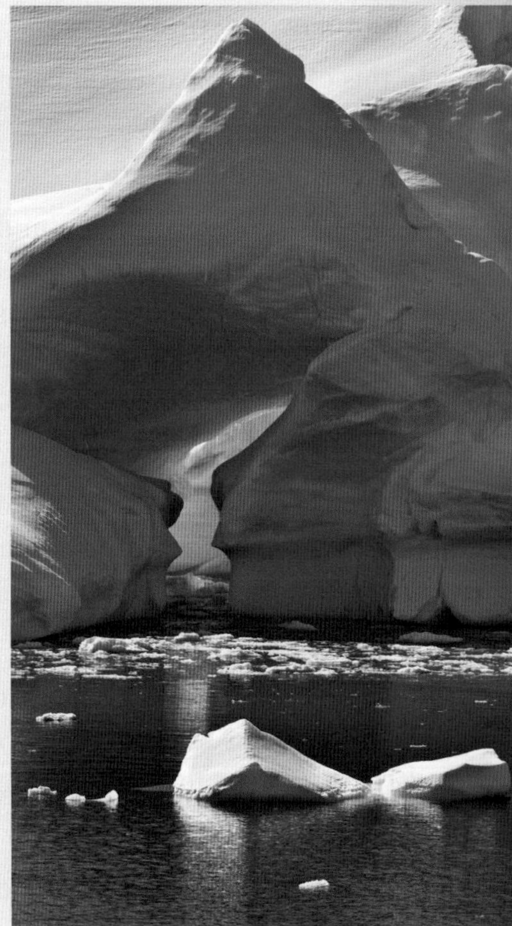

Follow up – understanding multiple-choice questions

Working on your own, now write your set of 12 multiple-choice questions.

For each question, a prompt below identifies the skills to be tested. You need to write a question to test that skill and give the right answer and some wrong answers, including a good distractor.

Questions on the first paragraph only

1. Write a question to test a literary technique used to persuade the reader in the first two sentences. (Hint: look at the adjectives.)
2. Write a question which tests explicit understanding of why Antarctica is so difficult to get to.
3 Write a vocabulary question to test understanding of an unusual adjective.

Questions on the second paragraph only

4. Write a vocabulary question to give an adjective which shows how carefully expeditions had to be planned in the past.
5. Write an understanding question to identify two explicit conditions under which tourists are allowed to visit Antarctica.
6. Write a punctuation question to identify how two words are joined together in this paragraph.

Questions on the third paragraph only

7. Write a vocabulary question, focused on an adjective which describes the harshness of the Antarctic winter.
8. Write a question to test grammar and identify the type of word used to describe the actions of whales and seals in the Antarctic summer. (Hint: you can either focus on verbs or adverbs.)
9. Write an understanding question which tests the changes in Antarctica which are implicit when winter turns to summer. This should be a two-mark question using 'your own words'.

Questions on the fourth paragraph only

10. Write a question to test the structural feature which introduces the different geographical areas covered by the continent of Antarctica.
11. Write a question to identify the literary technique that suggests rare wildlife is specially protected in Antarctica.
12. Write a question to test implicit understanding that an expedition to Antarctica is different from an ordinary cruise.

When you have finished, discuss your questions with your teacher.

Tip

Good multiple-choice questions need good distractors as well as a correct answer which is precise and cannot be contested. The length of the answers should be similar, as should their style. For example, if vocabulary is being tested, you only need to list the alternative words.

5 Exploration and investigation

In this unit, you will engage with what makes people want to explore and investigate different places – and perhaps themselves. You will read about journeys up the River Amazon and about a boy who swims with a dolphin, listen to students speaking about what motivates explorers, and discuss and plan expeditions of your own. You will use ideas and information about exploration and investigation to persuade others to support your own projects.

And in doing all that, you will be practising these key skills:

Speaking & Listening

- Organise ideas effectively for maximum impact on your audience in a talk about exploring yourself as well as other places.
- Take turns in discussion to achieve an agreed outcome about what items would most help you to survive when lost in the Amazon jungle.

Writing

- Adapt the features and conventions of informative and persuasive writing in order to create your own information texts and newspaper reports.
- Use a variety of sentence structures for impact on your readers.

Reading

- Recognise the features and style of informative and persuasive writing by focusing on the way different experiences of explorations are conveyed.
- Synthesise information from accounts of visits to the Amazonian region and develop evaluative skills to inform your own writing.

Assessment workshop

You will gain practice in the key assessment skills of reading and comparing texts of different types. You will respond to these texts by structuring your own longer pieces of writing, especially writing persuasively for greater impact.

Thinking time

Use the pictures on the opposite page and the quotations in speech bubbles to help you think about the following:

1. What words do you associate with the idea of exploration?
2. Do you know the difference between travel, exploration and adventure? Suggest a definition for each word.
3. Do you think it is possible to be an explorer in the traditional sense today? Where would you like to explore and why?

"These days there seems to be nowhere left to explore, at least on the land area of the Earth."
Carl Sagan

"Exploration is experiencing what you have not experienced before."
Richard Aldington

"Every new city or country or continent that I visit is a beautiful exploration from which I can learn."
Andrea Michaels

Speaking & Listening – exploring a short presentation

Exploration does not have to involve exploring a place – it could be about exploring ideas or experiences.

1. Working with a partner, give a short presentation to the class on ways you can explore and investigate without travelling anywhere. Is exploring the same as investigating? Consider this in your presentation.
2. As a class, be ready to give feedback to each pair on their presentation.

Features of different text types

You are going to be investigating a number of different text types. Below are some of the features of different text types.

includes a description of the setting — uses connectives to show a sequence of steps
has an address at the top — uses the present tense — has persuasive language
uses connectives to link arguments — has direct address to the reader
contains commands — has a headline — often written in the past tense
includes technical language — uses passive constructions — includes many adjectives
written in the third person — uses rhetorical questions — written in the first person

1. With a partner, make a list of as many different text types as you can.
2. On your own, choose one text type and make a list of its features. Use some of the suggestions above and add your own ideas.
3. Now share your ideas with your partner. Which features are common to different text types?

City of the beasts

This text is from a novel about a boy called Alex, who is on an expedition, exploring the Amazon on a boat with his grandmother, Kate, who is a writer.

The jungle loomed threateningly on both banks of the river. The captain's orders were clear: do not wander off for any reason; once among the trees, you lose your sense of direction. (…)

Time went by slowly, hours dragging into **eternity**; even so, Alex was never bored. He would sit at the prow of the boat and **observe** nature, and read, and play his grandfather's flute. The jungle seemed to come alive and respond to the sound of the instrument; even the noisy crew and the passengers on the boat would fall silent and listen. Those were the only times that Kate paid any attention to Alex. The writer was a woman of few words; she spent her day reading or writing in her notebooks (…) Everything about this trip was so different from the world Alex had grown up in that he felt like a visitor from another galaxy. Now he had to do without comforts he had always taken for granted, like a bed, a bathroom, running water, and electricity. (…)

douse	**queasy**
eternity	**radiant**
observe	**torrential**

Glossary

caboclos a Brazilian of mixed ancestry

His most serious problem was food. He had always been a picky eater, and now they were serving him things he couldn't even name. (...) One day the crew shot a couple of monkeys, and that night when the boat was tied up along the riverbank they were roasted. (...) Alex felt **queasy** just seeing them. The next morning they caught a *pirarucú*, an enormous fish that everyone but Alex, who didn't even taste it, thought was delicious. (...)

Several times a day a brief but **torrential** rain fell and the humidity was horrendous. Alex had to get used to the fact that his clothing never really got dry and that after the sun went down, they were attacked by clouds of mosquitoes. The foreigners' defence was to **douse** themselves in insect repellent (...). The *caboclos*, on the other hand, seemed immune to the bites.

On the third day, a **radiant** morning, they had to stop because there was a problem with the motor. While the captain tried to repair it, everyone else stretched out in the shade of the roof to rest. It was too hot to move, but Alex decided it was a perfect place to cool off. He jumped into the water, which looked as shallow as a bowl of soup, but he sank like a stone beneath the surface.

'Only an idiot tests the bottom with his feet,' Alex's grandmother commented when he came to the surface streaming water from his ears.

Alex swam away from the boat (...). He felt so comfortable that when something quickly brushed by his hand he took an instant to react. Not having any idea what kind of danger lay in store (...) he began to swim as fast as he could back toward the boat, but he stopped short when he heard his grandmother yelling not to move. (...) He floated as quietly as possible and then saw a huge fish at his side. He thought it was a shark, and his heart stopped, but the fish made a quick turn and came back, curious, coming so close that Alex could see its smile. This time his heart leaped, and he had to force himself not to shout with joy. He was swimming with a dolphin!

From *City of the Beasts* by Isabel Allende

Global Perspectives

Education is a right for all, yet in many places young people don't have opportunities to explore and investigate places beyond their own local area. Evaluate the difficulties young people face in learning more about themselves as a result of not being able to broaden their horizons by travelling and investigating other cultures.

Understanding

1. Find two words in the first paragraph which make the jungle sound dangerous.
2. The writer shows that there were aspects of the trip that Alex enjoyed and aspects which he didn't enjoy so much. Summarise in two lists the enjoyable and the less enjoyable aspects of the trip.
3. What impression do you get of Alex's grandmother, Kate? Support your ideas with quotations from the text.
4. How does the writer structure the final paragraph to build up to the last sentence?
5. Identify the features of this extract which show that it is from a narrative text.
6. Write the opening paragraph about a place you have visited, giving it a sense of danger.

Word builder

1. Look at the words in the Word cloud on page 88. How many of them do you know? Write a dictionary definition for one that you know the meaning of. Follow this pattern:

Selfie

- noun – plural 'selfies'
- informal
- a photograph that one takes of oneself, typically with a smartphone, and posts to a social media website
- origin early 21st century: from *self* + *-ie*.

Oxford English Dictionary

2. Have another look at the words you don't know the meaning of. Re-read the sentence where each one appears in the text. Try to work out from the context what each word means. Then check your answers in the dictionary. Add any words that are new to you to your personal vocabulary list.

Figurative language

Writers use figurative language to help create vivid pictures in the reader's imagination as they read. Figurative language includes:

- **Similes** – where something is compared to something else, using *like* or *as*
- **Metaphors** – where something is compared to something else, without using *like* or *as*
- **Personification** – where something is described as though it is a person/human
- **Alliteration** – where words which start with the same sound are deliberately placed together

Developing your language – identifying figurative language

1. Which of the following, from the text, is an example of a simile, personification or alliteration?

  a 'The jungle seemed to come alive and respond to the sound of the instrument'

  b 'He jumped into the water, which looked as shallow as a bowl of soup'

  c 'the humidity was horrendous'

2. Look at the section of text below. What do you notice about the length and structure of sentences the writer uses?

'Alex swam away from the boat (...). He felt so comfortable that when something quickly brushed by his hand he took an instant to react. Not having any idea what kind of danger lay in store (...) he began to swim as fast as he could back toward the boat, but he stopped short when he heard his grandmother yelling not to move.'

3. Look at the last sentence. The writer could have written:

He began to swim as fast as he could back toward the boat, not having any idea what kind of danger lay in store but he stopped short when he heard his grandmother yelling not to move.

How is the effect of this version different? Why do you think the writer chose to write the sentence in the way she did?

Explorers and expeditions

Why do people become explorers and go on expeditions? Is it exciting or terrifying, or both? Listen to the discussion between Adil and Nenet about exploration.

Listen to the audio for this task:

Understanding

1. Adil and Nenet have different views about explorers and exploring the world. Explain how their views are different.
2. Explain two ideas about people exploring remote places that they agree about.
3. What do the following quotations mean?
   - **a** 'go off and push the boundaries of what is possible'
   - **b** 'not making your mark on a place but allowing that place to make a mark on you'
4. Who did you agree with more – Nenet or Adil – and why?
5. Find examples of what Nenet and Adil say which show that they are listening to what each other says.
6. Has your opinion of exploration and investigation changed as a result of listening to this discussion?

Word cloud

addictive	**hostile**
countless	**new**
dangerous	**remote**
famous	**wonderful**

Developing your language – identifying sentence types

When we talk, we use a range of sentence types, which include statements, questions, commands and exclamations.

1. Match each of the following to a sentence type.
   - **a** 'I'd love to become an explorer, like Benedict Allen.'
   - **b** 'Why on Earth would anyone want to do this?'
   - **c** 'How awesome is that!'
   - **d** 'You are right about that.'
2. Why is it easy to spot questions and exclamations?
3. In speech, people don't always speak in complete sentences. Find three examples of incomplete sentences from the discussion between Adil and Nenet.
4. What other features of spoken English do you notice when you listen to Adil and Nenet? How is spoken English different from written English?

Remember

A rhetorical question, like *Hey, did you know?*, is a question directed at the reader or listener which does not expect an answer. It is designed to get the audience's attention, introduce an idea or make them think.

Word builder

Look at the words in the Word cloud. *Addictive* is an adjective which often has a negative meaning, as it may mean doing too much of something and not being able to stop even when the consequences could be harmful.

1. Name the word classes for the other words in the Word cloud. Look up definitions in a dictionary if any of the words is unfamiliar.
2. Divide the words into those that create a positive impact and those that create a negative impact. Are there any words which could be either positive or negative?
3. Can you spot any other words from the same word classes in Nenet and Adil's discussion?

Speaking & Listening – group discussion

1. Imagine you have got lost in the Amazon jungle. Decide as a group which six of the items in the box below would be most helpful in enabling you to survive. You have five minutes to come to a unanimous decision!
2. Now evaluate how effectively you collaborated to get this task done.

Global Perspectives

Language and communication are essential if we are to investigate the world through encounters with other people and avoid misunderstanding, confusion and conflict. There are examples of excellent global collaboration to raise awareness as a result of enquiry and investigation. However, there are also failures – factors that impede communication and collaboration.

Remember

We use language differently in speech and writing. Sentence boundaries are not as important in speech as they are in writing, because we can always explain what we mean.

Insect repellent
A compass
A map
Matches
A knife
A tarpaulin
A sleeping bag for each person
One pack of energy bars
Water purifying tablets
A cigarette lighter
A book on edible plants in the jungle
A mobile phone
A hammock for each person
A first aid kit
A spare change of clothes for each person

Varying your sentence structure for effect

It is important to use a range of sentences to make your writing interesting. This means using different sentence types, lengths and structures.

Below are some ways of varying your sentences. Sometimes this will affect the meaning; sometimes it will alter the emphasis or impact.

A. Changing the order of clauses in a coordinated sentence
Examples:

He was surprised and reached out to touch the dolphin.

He reached out to touch the dolphin and was surprised.

B. Changing the position of the subordinate clause in a complex sentence
Examples:

Although they sometimes take risks, explorers help us to understand more about the world we live in.

Explorers, although they sometimes take risks, help us to understand more about the world we live in.

Explorers help us to learn more about the world we live in, although they sometimes take risks.

C. Putting the subject near the end of the sentence

Examples:

In the depth of the water, several yards away from them lurked a massive alligator.

D. Starting with a non-finite/*-ing* verb

Examples:

Sweating, she pushed her way through the jungle.

Hiding behind a tree, he watched the elephant.

E. Starting with an adverb or adverbial

Examples:

Later, sitting round the campfire, they discussed the day's adventures.

For many weeks, they tried to rebuild their boat.

Now answer the following questions.

1. a What is the difference in meaning and effect between the two sentences under heading A opposite?

   b Try linking the clauses below in different ways, using different coordinating conjunctions: *and*, *but* and *or*. Look at the meaning and impact of each one. (You may find some don't really make sense!)

   Alex ate the fish Alex felt sick

2. a What is the difference in emphasis between the three sentences under heading B opposite?

   b Try rewriting the sentence below with the subordinate clause in different places. What is the effect in each case?

   It is difficult to find a part of the world that hasn't been explored, unless you are very determined.

3. a What is the effect of putting the subject at the end of the sentence? Try rewriting the sentence under heading C with the subject at the beginning. Does this sentence have a different effect?

   b Try writing two sentences with the subject at the end.

4. Try writing two sentences which start with a non-finite verb.
5. Try writing two sentences which start with an adverb or adverbial.
6. Now combine the clauses below into sentences. Aim to use some of the different structures you have been practising and try out different ways of combining the clauses.

the boat drifted	the trees whispered in the breeze
we drifted along the river	the trees looked as though they were moving
the river was deep	Alex leaned over the side
the river was dark	he saw an alligator
the river was mysterious	the alligator was sliding
on either side was the jungle	the alligator was sliding through the mud
the trees hung over the river	it looked as though it was smiling

Remember

There are lots of different ways to express your ideas in sentences. You can choose how you do this to create the effect you want.

Writing a newspaper article

You are going to write an article for a national newspaper about a group of young people who got lost while on a trek but managed to find their way back to safety.

You could include some of the following in your article:

- a summary of key information about what happened
- a more detailed account of what happened to the group of young people
- comments from the young people, their parents and other relevant people
- any other relevant information and ideas.

Begin by thinking about:

- the purpose and audience of the article
- the details of what happened – how many young people there were, how long were they lost for, what adventures they had
- the features of a newspaper article you want to include.

You also need to keep in mind the writing skills you will be assessed on:

- content, purpose and relevance to audience
- text structure
- sentence structure and punctuation
- spelling.

When writing an exercise such as this on paper, allocate some planning space to jot down your ideas and plan how you are going to organise your article. Remember, it is important to have effective first and last paragraphs as those are what the reader tends to remember.

You can plan your writing in a number of different ways. Here are some possible approaches.

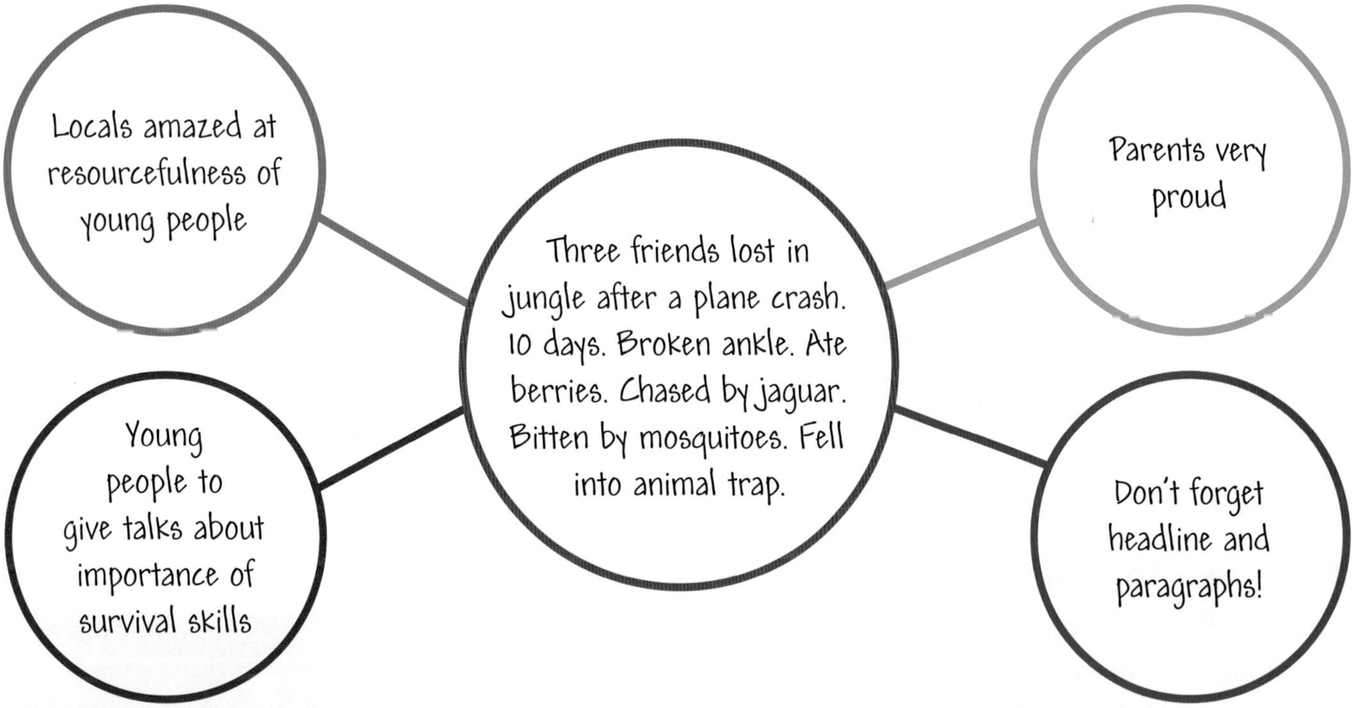

Three friends lost in jungle after a plane crash. 10 days. Broken ankle. Ate berries. Chased by jaguar. Bitten by mosquitoes. Fell into animal trap.

Locals amazed at resourcefulness of young people

Parents very proud

Young people to give talks about importance of survival skills

Don't forget headline and paragraphs!

Headline

Summarise main points – eight teenagers on school trip, wandered away from boat into jungle and couldn't find river, made a camp and fire and so on, found way back to river, boat gone but followed river to village to get help.

Main

Explain why they were on the trip, how they got lost, details of what happened (good and bad) with comments from teacher (left on boat), parents and one or more of the teenagers. Include comment from expert in survival?

Ending

How they got home, what they did next, what happened back at school, how future trips will make sure this doesn't happen again – safety arrangements.

Need to include a good ending that links back to the first paragraph

Now plan and write your article.

Remember

Be sure to follow the stages of the writing process:

- plan
- draft
- edit
- proofread.

In your writing remember to:

- use a variety of sentences
- punctuate comments as direct speech
- check spelling.

WB

Test the skills you have used in this unit on page 48 of the Workbook.

Establish

After you complete this section, you will be able to:

- ➔ recognise the key features of informative and persuasive writing
- ➔ synthesise information from texts to structure your directed writing
- ➔ evaluate your inferences and ideas, and develop them in your writing.

In an exam, you may be presented with two texts on a similar theme or topic but each with a different viewpoint and written in a different style. Here are two texts that illustrate this, relating to different experiences you could have in the Amazon rainforest.

Text A

First man to hike Amazon River ends his trek

British explorer Ed Stafford finished his two-year, 4,000-mile trek along the Amazon River on Monday, completing a feat never before accomplished (…). The hike, which he started at Camana, Peru, on 2 April 2008, ended Monday at Maruda Beach, Brazil.

Four months after he started, he was joined by Peruvian forestry worker Gadiel 'Cho' Sanchez Rivera. Sanchez intended only to guide Stafford for five days through a dangerous area near Satipo, Peru, but stayed to the end of the expedition. (…)

"I'm more tired and more elated than I've ever been in my life," Stafford said (…). "We've lived through some very serious situations and there have been times when we genuinely feared for our lives, but we never ever thought of giving up. The fact that everyone told us it was impossible spurred us on.

"At first it was terrifying but it's changed in our eyes during the expedition and a place that was once mysterious and dangerous to us is now a place where we feel safe. (…) It's not a scary place for us now; it's beautiful; we've fallen in love with it. (…)"

Despite collapsing from exhaustion on a roadside Sunday morning, Stafford had been confident he would finish in time Monday to catch a scheduled flight home (…).

It's the kind of fortitude that Stafford has summoned time and again since setting out from the Amazon River's source to raise international attention about rain-forest destruction and to help raise funds to combat it. (…)

Adapted from www.edition.cnn.com

Glossary

feat an achievement which requires great courage, skill or strength

fortitude courage when facing difficulties

spurred urged on by

Text B

Experience an Amazon rainforest family adventure in Peru!

Peru's Amazon rainforest is the perfect adventure playground for families looking for an educational and exciting holiday.

Our family programmes for kids – choose from 3, 4, 5 days or longer – focus on being educational and entertaining at the same time, and suitable for both children and their parents.

Kids can explore trails around the comfortable eco-lodge, following the story of a six-year-old girl (…) called Ania. Adults are welcome to join in, but can also choose to do their own activities.

The lodge, comfortable, accessible and well-designed, is built on a private reserve on the Tambopata National Reserve. It is becoming integrated into the communities of Brazil nut extractors, to extend the benefits of ecotourism.

It's the perfect destination for families wishing to explore and enjoy Peru's Amazon rainforest!

Adapted from www.responsibletravel.com

Glossary

Brazil nut extractors people who extract oil from Brazil nuts

ecotourism tourism which supports the conservation of places and their wildlife

Engage

Having read texts A and B, answer the following questions, which will help you carry out a compare and contrast analysis.

1. In what way is the first paragraph in Text A typical of a newspaper article?
2. Explain two ways you can tell Stafford's achievement in Text A was remarkable.
3. Apart from the first paragraph, identify the features of Text A that are typical of a newspaper article.
4. Why do you think the writer of Text B uses the phrase 'adventure playground' in the first paragraph?
5. Explain three ways Text B tries to appeal to parents.
6. What do you notice about the first and last paragraphs in Text B?

Tip

Non-narrative writing needs careful planning. Remember FLAP: format, language, audience, purpose. Use a style and language suitable for the format. An article is more formal than a speech and less formal than a letter. Engage with your audience and present plenty of facts and details to support informative writing.

Evaluate

Here are three responses to the task: Write an article about exploring the Amazon. Which writer would you like to offer some constructive and detailed advice to?

Tip

Consider how well each of these responses matches the purpose of the task, sustains an appropriate tone and is well organised. Is the response consistent and clear? Does it demonstrate good style and accuracy?

Alex

Lost in the jungle

Eight teenagers were on a school expotition to the Amason jungle and wandered away from their boat. This shows how dangerous these trips really are. Where were the teachers? Probably drinking coffe. The teacher said that it was typical of these teenagers they never do what they are told. I want deeper and deeper into the jungle and had the coolest experiences with tarantalas and piranhas and even swum with a dolfin

We met some really cool Indians they drink wierd stuff, we tried it and felt sick. Then one of the teachers found us and said it tort us a lesson. When we got back to school we were told how lucky we had been and that the school only wanted to take responsible people on trips so we better learn from this about listening to what we are told to do. I thought it was cool though and found out more by being with my mates.

Nadia

Lost in the Amazon

A group of kids were travelling in the Amazon when they get lost. This happened because they were looking at some insects, they forgot to follow the leader. This was because they saw some amazing butterflies as they were walking along. Their parents were very worried, they didn't know what to do. 'I am hoping my son is safe said one mother.' She wanted to go and look for him in the Amazon.

In the end the young people were safe. They kept by the river. They ate flowers and looked after each other. When they are arriving back to the city yesterday. It all ended happily.

It was a frightening experience. I was really scared and didn't know what to do. We decided to keep together and we made a camp, we caught some fish for food. We lit a fire so people could see us and we were lost for three days. One day, we had a good idea and we followed a river to get home.

Tomasz

Amazing Amazon Adventure!

On Friday 7th November a group of students from City College got lost in Amazon jungle. They had to use their survival skills to make their way back to camp and meet up with the rest of the group. They did this and it was all fine in the end.

It started one evening; when two students, Lia and Sen were drawn into the jungle by the strange sound of an animal. What could it be, they were thinking. So they decided to go and have a look. After a while, they realised they couldn't see any of the rest of the students. Then two other students who heard them shouting came after them and then they got lost too. The girls were crying and they didn't know what to do.

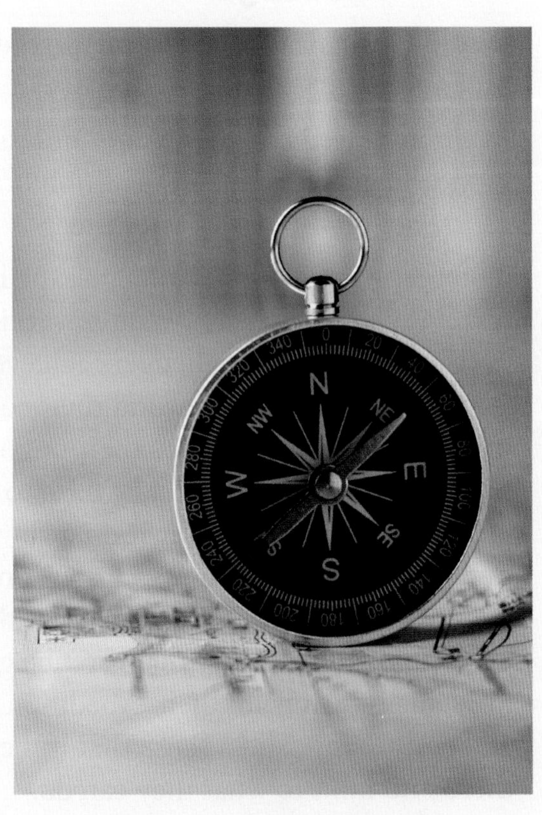

Suddenly, one of them said 'I have a compass. We can use this to find our way back to the river. They made a kind of tent to sleep in overnight and the next day they used the compass to find the river. 'It was scary but awesome,' says Lia, but her mother says that 'she wants to go travelling again'!

Enable

At the beginning of this Assessment workshop, one of your targets was to develop the quality of your directed writing.

Read this extract about expeditions provided for schools.

World Challenge

World Challenge is the leading provider of life-changing school expeditions.

From increased confidence and fitness to global awareness and money management, an expedition brings benefits that will have an impact on the rest of your life.

Completing a World Challenge expedition is an educational travel experience that goes on rewarding students, long after they return home. Challengers achieve more than they thought possible by stretching beyond their comfort zone, and this sense of accomplishment colours their ongoing view of themselves and their place in the world. They have to raise the bar in terms of physical fitness, communication, teamwork and organisation, all highly valuable skills they can draw on in their post-expedition lives. Engaging with another culture during the Project phase brings global awareness that can't be gleaned from books. Students return from their expedition with increased energy and enthusiasm, and a sense that if they really apply themselves, there's no limit to what they can do.

From World Challenge website

Tip

When longer pieces of writing are assessed, there are marks for the reading and evaluation of the texts as well as for the quality of your writing. Try to make inferences as you read, based on the information and viewpoints provided, and develop those ideas as you write your own piece.

Follow up – writing a persuasive letter

Respond to the following task.

Your school will sponsor eight students from your year group to go on a World Challenge. You will explore and investigate different parts of the world and perhaps learn more about yourselves by doing so.

Write a persuasive letter to the school leadership team to convince them that you should be one of the eight chosen students.

You should consider:

- the personal qualities which make you a suitable explorer and investigator
- how you will match the sponsorship funds through your own fundraising
- what you think you will learn about yourself by doing the challenge
- what you will contribute to the school community on your return.

Begin your letter by addressing the Leadership Team and end it by expressing the hope that they will select you as a lucky investigator.

Tip

Remember all the features that a persuasive letter requires, such as a formal tone, organised paragraphs, polite rhetorical features and a strong concluding recommendation. You will also need to check and proofread your letter carefully and ensure that it has a good mix of information and persuasion.

When you have finished, discuss your letter with your teacher.

6 Science and the future

In this unit, you will engage with how science will shape our future world. You will read about a project to make us all smarter and about plans for future space travel. You will listen to a student presenting the early life story of an inspirational figure. You will develop your vocabulary and ability to link ideas in order to present a powerful argument of your own about how learning might change in a future world.

And in doing all that, you will be practising these key skills:

Speaking & Listening

- Sustain a well-organised talk on teaching and learning in the future.
- Work with partners to challenge arguments about schools today, taking turns in order to improve each other's presentations.

Writing

- Make deliberate choices of vocabulary and structure arguments in order to enhance the impact of your writing.
- Evaluate arguments and counter-arguments when presenting your view in a magazine article.

Reading

- Evaluate the impact of a writer's presentation of language and arguments on whether listening to Mozart's music increases people's intelligence.
- Analyse the structure and organisational features of a text about space tourism in order to evaluate bias and its effect on readers.

Assessment workshop

You will gain practice in the key assessment skill of giving a short individual talk. You will structure and organise a talk about how teaching and learning might look in the future. You will also prepare for questions about your talk, so that you can discuss issues and extend your facts, ideas and opinions.

Thinking time

Our future world will be driven by science and technology.

1. Why has the world today become more dependent on science and technology?
2. Suggest which discoveries are most likely to change our world in the future.
3. What single change could make our future world a better place?
4. How can our learning in schools adapt to future challenges?

"For to be free is not merely to cast off one's chains, but to live in a way that respects and enhances the freedom of others."
Nelson Mandela

Teaching and learning in the future will be flipped. Turned upside down. Learners will become their own teachers having much more freedom than ever before.

Intellectual intelligence is the first step to freeing ourselves from our physical bonds. To really be free we must all make the most of our intelligence.

Speaking & Listening – rebranding your school

Your school has decided it needs to update the way it presents itself to parents and students in order to be more modern, diverse and inclusive. Its new branding will suggest it prepares students for the world of the future. It will also emphasise the school's reputation for teaching science.

1. You are going to design a new motto and logo for your school.
   - **a** What motto would sum up the values of your school, using no more than five words? Discuss and reach agreement.
   - **b** Discuss how a logo and brand can look more modern, look to the future and reflect the motto and values of your school.
   - **c** Consider:
     - how to relate the logo to the name of the school and your motto
     - whether you might adapt your current logo and brand
     - what colours to use.
2. Now design the logo for the school website, signs and stationery.
3. Prepare a short group presentation to share your ideas on what your logo represents and how the school should use it.

A balanced argument?

Unlocking the 'Mozart effect'

Almost everyone has heard of Mozart, but did you know that he was an accomplished pianist and violinist by the age of five? Not only that, but he began composing symphonies soon after and had completed over 600 works by the time of his death at only 35. There is no doubting that Mozart was a musical genius, but in recent times a theory has come to light that suggests his music might inspire genius in others.

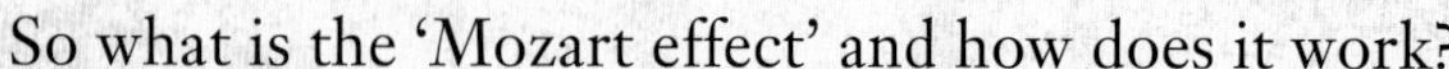

So what is the 'Mozart effect' and how does it work? It is a phrase that was coined by renowned otolaryngologist and inventor Alfred A. Tomatis in the early 1990s, and later developed as a theory by US music critic and teacher Don Campbell. Writing in the journal *Nature*, Campbell **theorised** that brain power could be increased as a result of listening to Mozart and demonstrated this with higher IQ scores in a test group. Although the effect was only temporary, it was enough to **arouse** widespread attention.

After all, who wouldn't want to be smarter given half the chance? The study certainly captured the interest of the mass media, and was soon reported widely and viewed by many who read about it as entirely **plausible**. It proved particularly popular with parents of young children, perhaps hopeful that they might have a prodigy in the making if their child listened to enough **sonatas** before bedtime. In the US, it was reported that the Governor of Georgia wished to allocate public funds so that children born in the state would be sent a classical music CD. The magic of Mozart was truly casting its spell.

In the years that followed, right up to today, the 'Mozart effect' has remained a popular theory, even though research has not always come out in its favour. For every study that claims improved **spatial** reasoning, there are just as many that point out flaws and lack of foundation in the original logic. Where effects have been observed, they are only temporary and, some might say, of minimal use. However,

Word cloud

arouse	**sonatas**
cortical	**spatial**
plausible	**theorised**

Glossary

come to light to be discovered, and widely shared

mass media newspapers, television, the Internet, radio and magazines

otolaryngologist a physician specialising in ear, nose and throat diseases and disorders

prodigy a highly talented young person

most experiments have been carried out on adults rather than children, and it has often been said that, by the time we reach adulthood, our capacity to learn is not as great as it once was.

Where does that leave us today? As recently as 2015, the *Daily Mail* reported that researchers from the Sapienza University of Rome had linked listening to Mozart with improved memory function in young adults and the elderly. Interestingly, there were no such effects in those who listened to Beethoven, leading the researchers to speculate that particular patterns in Mozart's music 'activated' **cortical** circuits of the brain. Furthermore, in a separate study by the University of Electronic Science and Technology of China, rodents with epilepsy were exposed to the music of Mozart and their mental processing vastly improved as a result, which could suggest a positive application for humans with a similar condition.

Perhaps that means there is something in the 'Mozart effect' after all? It would be good to think that even now, more than 300 years after his death, Wolfgang Amadeus Mozart is helping others through his music. And even if it can't make everyone who listens to it instantly smarter, at least we can enjoy it for what it is – beautiful, timeless music.

Understanding

In the article, the writer considers whether the 'Mozart effect' has an effect on our level of intelligence.

1. In your own words, what is the 'Mozart effect'?
2. Who was Mozart?
3. Why were the particular patterns in Mozart's music thought to have an effect on the brain?
4. In what ways did people react to the original study, and why?
5. Do you think the writer believes in the 'Mozart effect'? Explain your reasoning.
6. Can you think of other things we do that are likely to stimulate intelligence?

Global Perspectives

Intelligence can be defined as the ability to gain knowledge and apply skills. Artificial intelligence, known as AI, suggests that human intelligence can be re-created by machines. But doesn't human intelligence go beyond anything machines can achieve? Can you think of examples, locally and globally, where human intelligence is valued, and also where different kinds of intelligence are being used?

Word builder

Low-frequency words are considered to be more difficult to understand and are used less by writers.

All six words in the Word cloud would be considered of low frequency.

Sometimes the meaning of more difficult words can be identified because they look and sound like root words which are more commonly used. Also, the context can offer clues to the meaning of a difficult word. For example, you might explore the meaning of *spatial* in this way:

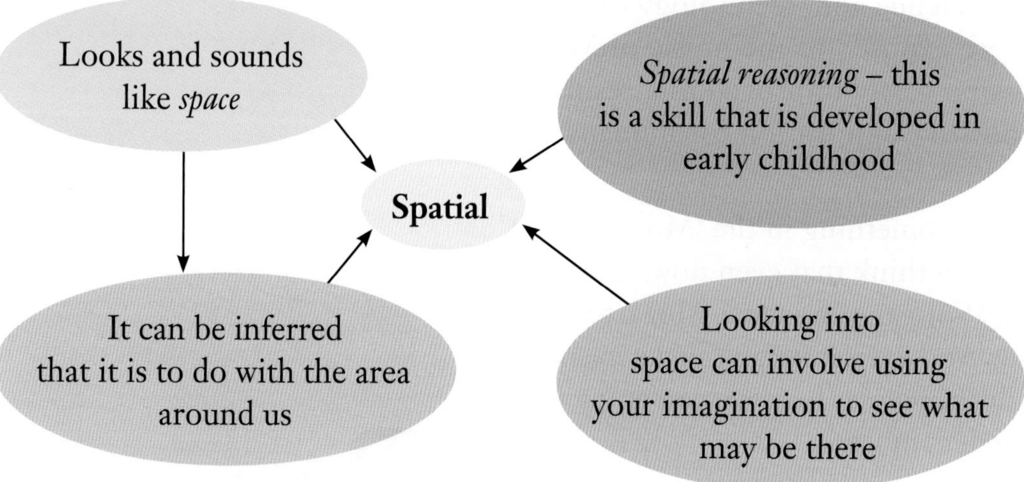
Looks and sounds like *space*
Spatial reasoning – this is a skill that is developed in early childhood
Spatial
It can be inferred that it is to do with the area around us
Looking into space can involve using your imagination to see what may be there

Indeed, ***spatial reasoning*** tests require students to mentally rotate and re-order objects without being able to physically touch them.

1. Use the same process but, instead of *spatial*, apply it to the word *theorised*.
2. Can this process be used for any of the other four words in the Word cloud? Give reasons for your answers.
3. Use a dictionary to look up the precise meaning of *cortical* and *sonata*.
   a What more common terms could be used in their place?
   b How would the use of the more common terms detract from their meaning in the passage?

Remember

One of the ways you can make your writing more effective is to expand your vocabulary and use a wider range of words. Used correctly, low-frequency words help to create a more mature writing style.

Developing your writing – using topic sentences

A topic sentence:
- is the first sentence in a paragraph
- introduces the main idea in the paragraph.

A topic sentence is useful because:
- it focuses the writing within the paragraph
- it acts as a summary of the points in the paragraph.

This is the first sentence in the article.

'Almost everyone has heard of Mozart, but did you know that he was an accomplished pianist and violinist by the age of five?'

It is an effective opening because:
- 'Almost everyone has heard of' suggests you have prior knowledge because this subject is important enough to be well known.
- 'but did you know' involves the reader by leading them into the topic and presenting an interesting fact.
- 'an accomplished pianist and violinist by the age of five?' introduces the main theme of the article with an example of a child genius.

The rest of the paragraph consists of two related sentences.

Sentence	Writer suggests	Reader
2	Mozart achieved much in his short lifetime	reflects on what they have achieved or might achieve in that time
3	Mozart's music inspires genius in others	is interested in whether it could have that effect on them

1. Write down a list of topic sentences for the rest of the article.
2. Look at the last paragraph beginning 'Perhaps that means…'. Copy and complete the table below to show how the paragraph is developed.

Sentence	Writer suggests	Reader
1	The 'Mozart effect' might have some truth to it	Reflects on what they have read in the article
2	It is a good thing because it helps those who need it	

Remember

Topic sentences can be used to introduce paragraphs in all kinds of writing, including argumentative, persuasive and narrative.

Writing a series of topic sentences can be an effective way of planning a piece of writing.

Space tourism

How to prepare for a holiday in space

How is that for a holiday destination? Travel in a small group for great, arguably **unrivalled** views from a height of more than 100 kilometres above Earth. Even experience weightlessness. Granted, the trip to outer space will last just a few minutes, but the promise that tourists can soon 'earn their astronaut wings' is becoming ever more real.

In November 2015, private spaceflight company Blue Origin performed a **historic** feat: it launched, flew and successfully landed a **reusable** rocket carrying the company's New Shepard space vehicle.

Virgin Galactic with its SpaceShipTwo rocket ship also wants to take private citizens beyond the atmosphere, as do XCOR Aerospace and Space Adventures, among others. Space tourism finally seems set to take off, with hundreds of people having put down **hefty** deposits to secure places on the first few commercial passenger spacecraft.

Per Wimmer is one of them. The 47-year-old Danish financier and entrepreneur has been waiting for his chance to go to space for more than 16 years, with tickets from Virgin Galactic, Space Adventures and XCOR in his pocket since the early 2000s.

Preparation

So how does one get ready to go to space, apart from finding the **chunky** sum of money to pay for the ticket? Your body will need **rigorous** training to survive the immense stress of space travel, and Wimmer has done it all, from floating in simulated zero gravity and piloting fighter jets, to spinning in a centrifuge.

Among the commercial space companies, it's also worth mentioning SpaceX and its founder, Elon Musk. The firm's Falcon 9 rocket has different aims, doing orbital flights rather than the sub-orbital trip that Wimmer hopes to accomplish. Falcon 9 has already delivered cargo to the International Space Station, while last December SpaceX successfully managed to land its first reusable rocket in an upright position. "They are doing fantastically well, but still it'll be years before they'll take humans up there," says Wimmer.

Feel the force

So, will all space tourists have to go through a training programme as rigorous as the one Wimmer subjected himself to? Well, he says, a centrifuge and a zero-g test are a must. "You do need the centrifuge to really feel the g-forces on your body, because the moment you go up, it really hits you. And if you haven't trained, you'll get a bit of a shock and you won't enjoy the trip as much."

By Katia Moskvitch, *Engineering and Technology*

Understanding

1. Which five companies were actively preparing to take ordinary people into space when this article was written?
2. What kind of preparation is necessary for a flight in space?
3. According to Per Wimmer, why are Elon Musk's ambitions going to take longer to achieve?
4. Why do you think the writer introduces Wimmer and his experiences?
5. What do you think would be the most worthwhile form of space travel for tourists and what are the criteria needed to achieve this?
6. Imagine you are the leader of your country. Right now, would you approve a multi-billion dollar investment in space travel? Write some notes for a speech you intend to make to your government.

Word builder

Choice of adjectives can emphasise the excitement but also the strenuousness of preparing for the future.

1. Look at each of the adjectives in the Word cloud. Do they stress the excitement of space travel or its difficulties? Could any of these words be used for both?
2. Convert four of these adjectives into adverbs, and write a sentence to illustrate the use of each new word.
3. Find where the article uses the words *successfully* and *finally*. What do these words convey to you about what has been achieved in this field so far?
4. **a** What technique does the writer use to structure the article?

   b Is it an objective article or do the adjectives and adverbs indicate bias?

Global Perspectives

Space travel offers the possibility of migration and settlement in space or on other planets. Migration seems to be increasing in the world today and has successes and failures globally. Is your local or regional area impacted by migration or immigration? Do you think countries will collaborate on creating communities in space?

Glossary

centrifuge a spinning machine subjecting pilots and astronauts to high forces of acceleration to simulate the effect of zero-gravity

earn their astronaut wings pilots are said to earn their wings when they qualify to fly solo

orbital flight the spacecraft needs to make at least one flight around Earth which currently requires rocket launch to move beyond Earth's atmosphere

sub-orbital does not complete a full orbit of the Earth (or other celestial body).

weightlessness absence of the sensation of weight in space, also called zero gravity or zero-g

Word cloud

chunky	**reusable**
hefty	**rigorous**
historic	**unrivalled**

Transitions

Transitions are words and phrases used to connect ideas in writing. They are often linked with connectives because they have similar roles in written work.

Example:

Space tourism finally seems set to take off, with hundreds of people having put down hefty deposits to secure places on the first few commercial passenger spacecraft.

Here the transition is *finally* because it moves from the dream of space tourism to practicalities, including people who have already paid for their tickets.

Transitions are used to:

Order/sequence ideas
e.g. first of all
secondly
finally

Show cause and effect
e.g. consequently
as a result
hence

Add information
e.g. in addition
furthermore
moreover

Indicate place
e.g. beyond
in the background
adjacent to

Indicate time
e.g. presently
subsequently
immediately

Compare
e.g. equally
similarly
in the same way

Contrast
e.g. and yet
on the contrary
alternatively

Give examples/show emphasis/illustrate
e.g. namely
in particular
illustrated by

Conclude
e.g. to conclude
to summarise
on the whole

Identifying transitions

Identify the transition in these sentences which describe the work of a humanitarian organisation called Médicins Sans Frontières (MSF), or Doctors Without Borders.

1. Médecins Sans Frontières is guided by strong medical ethics in addition to a desire to help all people.
2. MSF raised millions of dollars from appeals last year and subsequently helped millions of people.
3. The positive effect that MSF has achieved can be illustrated by the awards it has gathered worldwide.

Why transitions are important

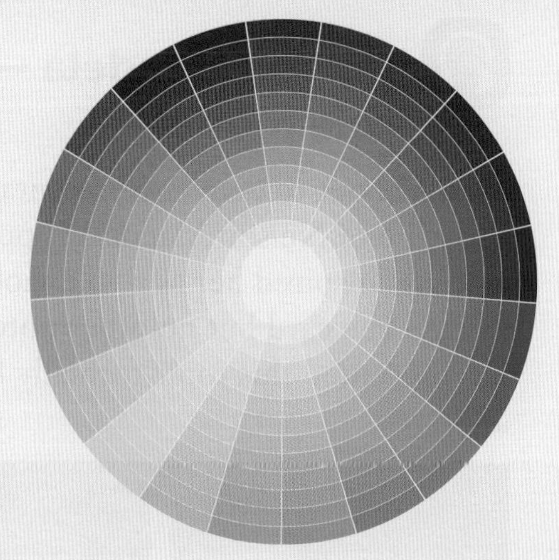

The difference between transitions and connectives is that transitions define more closely the connection between ideas in your writing.

Look at these two simple statements about charities:

They need money. They help people.

Now add two transitions:

***First** they need money **then** they help people.*

Using *first* and *then* enables the reader to clearly understand the order of events.

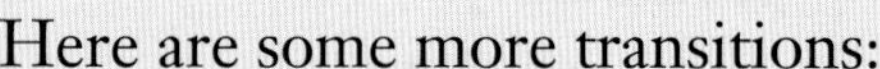

Here are some more transitions:

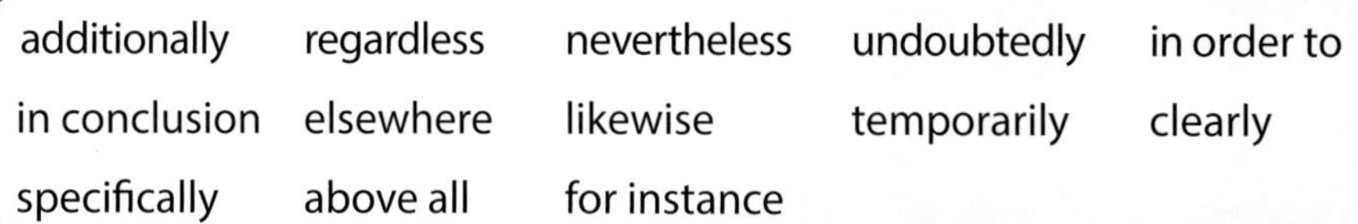

additionally	regardless	nevertheless	undoubtedly	in order to
in conclusion	elsewhere	likewise	temporarily	clearly
specifically	above all	for instance		

1. Copy and complete the statements by using appropriate transitions from the box. All of the transitions have been used once.

a The doctors treated the wounded __________ of the shells falling around them. __________ the nurses were also in danger.

b __________ save lives __________ the charity has to be well organised.

c Helping refugees, __________ in Sudan, __________ relieves their suffering; __________ a more permanent solution is needed.

d Doctors give their services free of charge but __________ the medicines they use are very expensive so funds must be raised __________ and __________ by using the Internet. __________ the cost of transporting aid to where it is needed is expensive so, while the doctors are working, support workers are trying to raise funds.

e __________ I would say that MSF does a wonderful job.

2. Make a list of all the transitions mentioned on this page.

a Look through the written work you have done over the last seven days and add a tick by each transition every time you used it.

b When you have completed your review, consider whether you are using enough transitions in your writing or whether you should be using more.

Nelson Mandela – an inspiring role model

Listen to the audio for this task:

Sara is about to deliver a presentation to her teacher on the early life of Nelson Mandela, a political leader in South Africa who has inspired her as a role model for the future. She is using a cue card but no other notes. This is the first time she has presented this topic formally but she has been practising at home.

Word cloud

admittedly
essentially
frankly
predictably
understandably
undoubtedly

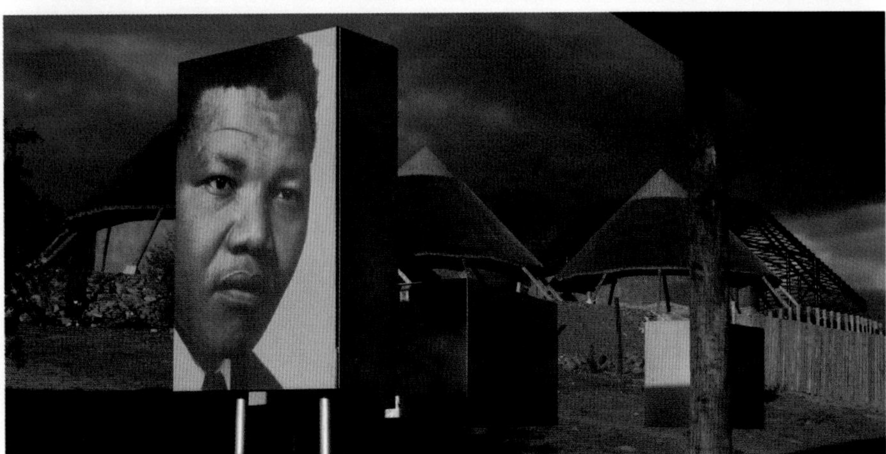

Understanding

1. What was Nelson Mandela's given first name at birth?
2. Where was Nelson Mandela born?
3. Which two incidents in his early adulthood showed that Nelson Mandela was not afraid to challenge authority if he thought his cause was just?
4. Although the presentation is based on a serious subject, Sara is not afraid to use humour in her responses in the discussion. How does she do this?
5. Can you think of a person from your own country who sets an example in a similar way to Nelson Mandela? Explain your choice wth examples.

   What are the personal qualities they have shown which make them inspiring figures for your future?
6. You are going to speak for five minutes about a well-known, global celebrity who you are recommending as an ambassador for the future. Who will it be and why?

Glossary

African National Congress a political party in South Africa

apartheid a system of segregation based on ethnic origin

cue card brief notes used as an aid to memory

kraal a homestead surrounded by a wall

rondavel a round hut made of soil baked into bricks

Developing your language – using discourse markers

Although discourse markers can appear in different forms of writing, they are more often found in examples of both formal and informal speech. Generally, if the discourse marker is removed from the phrase, the sentence will still be grammatically correct.

Discourse markers are used:

- to begin a topic in a conversation – *'Right, I want to talk about Mandela.'*
- to refocus a conversation – *'on the other hand'*
- as fillers or to delay speaking – *'you know'*, *'well'*
- to offer minimal feedback during a conversation dominated by the speaker – *'exactly'*, *'absolutely'*, *'yes, I agree'*
- to focus attention on what is to come in the sentence – *'As far as I am concerned...'*.

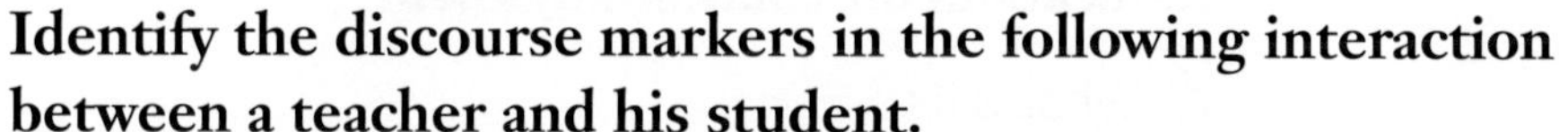

Identify the discourse markers in the following interaction between a teacher and his student.

"Now then, we've all heard of Nelson Mandela but on the other hand how many of you knew his given first name was Rolihlahla? How about you Rohit, did you know?" Amid much shaking of heads from the rest of the class, Rohit timidly replied. "No sir, well, I always thought it was Nelson, you know, because that's what they call him on the news channel, please sir. As far as I am concerned, that's his name, sir."

Remember

Discourse markers can be very effective when they are used appropriately or very distracting when they are not, so it is important to recognise them.

Word builder

The words in the Word cloud are also discourse markers, signalling the attitude or point of view being expressed.

Copy the lists and match the six words to the correct attitude or point of view intended.

a	Definite, without question	Admittedly
b	Expected, given the circumstances	Essentially
c	Logically, based on what is known	Frankly
d	Confessing agreement	Predictably
e	Being honest and plain speaking	Understandably
f	Expressed in a basic way	Undoubtedly

Writing an effective argument

You are going to write a six-paragraph argumentative essay for the school's magazine, exploring this question:

'Should pupils be able to listen to music whilst studying in class?'

Planning your response

Use these boxes to guide you. They do not necessarily have to be completed in this order.

Consider the question

- ✓ Decide where you stand on this subject.
- ✓ Think of four points in support of your opinion.

Consider the target audience

- ✓ Adopt a suitable tone – provocative/dismissive/pleading?

Form your topic sentences

- ✓ Turn your four points into four topic sentences.
- ✓ This will be the main body of your essay.

Think about the counter-argument

- ✓ What is it?
- ✓ How is it weaker?
- ✓ What proof can you use?

Opening paragraph

- ✓ Practise some introductory sentences.
- ✓ Aim for something that grabs the reader's attention.

Concluding paragraph

- ✓ Have a clear idea about where you stand on the question.
- ✓ Aim for a memorable last sentence.

The "Prove it!" game

Play the game using the following rules.

1. Player 1 states a point.
2. Player 2 challenges by shouting "Prove it!"
3. Player 1 then has to offer evidence to support his/her point.
4. If Player 2 is not satisfied, he/she continues to shout "Prove it!" until sufficient evidence is provided.

Writing frame

Paragraph 1 – introduction

- Begin with a strong comment.
- Give an overview of the argument, introducing the four points you are going to use to support your opinion.
- Make sure the reader is aware of how you stand on the question.

Paragraphs 2–4

- In turn, expand on the four ideas introduced in your opening paragraph.
- Prove your opinion.
- Consider one point per paragraph.
- Introduce each with a topic sentence stating the key point.
- The rest of each paragraph should prove the key point.

Paragraph 5 – counter-argument

- Introduce the counter-argument.
- Explain why it isn't as strong as your argument.

Conclusion

- Sum up your argument.
- End with a strong comment that the reader will remember.
- Link back to opening points.
- Ensure your viewpoint is consistent with that expressed in the introductory paragraph.

Remember to use

Transitions

Topic sentences

Low-frequency words

Remember

When making a point:

- Clearly state the point.
- Support it with evidence to provide proof.
- Offer an explanation that backs up the evidence.

WB

Test the skills you have used in this unit on page 57 of the Workbook.

Establish

After you complete this section, you will be able to:

- ➔ deliver a spoken presentation promoting your own viewpoint with confidence
- ➔ skilfully manage the language and structure of your talk to achieve maximum impact
- ➔ evaluate your own talk and that of others, learning how to handle questions and feedback.

In some ways designing a sustained talk is the same as writing a longer essay:

- The goal is to successfully communicate a series of connected ideas to the audience.
- The text is written in sentences that are grammatically correct enough to express meaning.
- The text is divided into paragraphs that each deal with a separate point and, ideally, are introduced using topic sentences.
- Success is based on the quality of the content and how well it is presented to the audience.

It is the delivery that differs:

- Written texts are delivered through the indirect medium of words on a page punctuated effectively so the reader can create the voice of the writer internally.
- Oral presentations create a direct link between the presenter and the audience.

Tip

Questions can be used to prompt answers that provide factual information. They can also take the form of rhetorical questions, encouraging us to evaluate content and present our own opinions. Use questions as discourse markers in your talk, both to present facts and to encourage your listeners to think.

Engage

Complete the following tasks to help you prepare for a suitable talk. This skill will be useful for speaking assessments in future examinations.

1. Create two columns headed 'Engaging' and 'Unengaging'. With the audience in mind, work out which characteristics of a talk, in the box on the right, belong in each column.

lively	one-paced
dull	monotonous
rehearsed	considered
fluent	rushed
thoughtful	articulate

read from a script
a range of intonation
a range of linguistic devices
discourse markers
important points emphasised

2. You have been tasked with designing a five-minute talk on one of the following:
   - How science and technologies will change our futures
   - How we should prepare for our future world.

   Write an opening paragraph for your talk. This will involve planning and organising your ideas.
3. Present your opening paragraph and listen carefully to the resulting observations regarding how engaging it is.
4. Now write the rest of the talk.
5. Prepare your talk to be delivered at some point in the future. You do not need to deliver it now. Practise informally, using a range of intonation. Note any mistakes you make and areas you feel need amending.

Preparing for the discussion

After you have delivered your talk, you are likely to be asked to discuss the content. This discussion could last for five minutes so detailed responses are required.

Although you will not know what questions will be asked and what direction the discussion will take, you can have some control over it.

- Think of five or six questions that might be asked about the content of your talk. Think about your answers to each one. Try to extend these answers to last for 20–30 seconds each.
- Often the questions asked will be a direct result of what you say in the discussion, so only introduce points if you are willing to discuss them.
- Don't be passive and wait for the next question. Ask your own questions and be prepared to fill pauses with your own comments.

Open and closed questions

The response will always depend on the kind of question asked.

Closed questions are easier to answer but difficult to expand beyond the basic response. 'Do you believe students should control their own learning?' is a closed question as it requires a 'yes' or 'no' response.

Open questions are more effective as they allow you to offer opinions and expand upon your initial answer. 'Why is having a role in designing your own learning important to you?' is an open question as it doesn't have a 'yes' or 'no' answer.

Tip

You will be assessed for your listening skills as well as your speaking skills, so practise listening carefully to the views of others, giving them time to express themselves, and then respond appropriately. It's usually a good idea to develop the points they make as this demonstrates empathy.

Tip

It's a good idea to hold back a couple of facts and examples on cue card notes and not deliver them in the talk. Try to predict the areas that your listener will want to pursue and develop, then you can use your saved notes effectively and relevantly in the discussion.

Evaluate

Three students are planning their five-minute talks. Below are the openings from their talks. Using the criteria in the white box, decide on the relative merits of each opening.

- ✓ Planned and structured for effectiveness
- ✓ Appropriate for the target audience
- ✓ Offers a balanced and considered argument
- ✓ Level of vocabulary is challenging
- ✓ Tone is measured and analytical
- ✓ Persuasive
- ✓ Engaging for an audience

Vocabulary is sophisticated and effective. Can the student maintain this high level? Remember that the vocabulary has to fit the intended meaning, as it does here

Ali

As long as schools continue to exist we will continue to debate the efficacy of school preparation for our future lives. Many will see schools as a way of preparing students for adult life beyond the classroom and recognise that the knowledge instilled will engender a respect for authority and a self-disciplined approach to study that will stand us in good stead in our adult lives. Others will continue to view the curriculum as old-fashioned, unnecessary and designed to subjugate independent spirit and innovation. However, I believe these latter harbingers of doom and destruction to be in the minority. Most students just want to succeed in their academic studies, and see the school curriculum as teaching them a love of learning for its own sake. To quote Mr Hector in 'The History Boys', 'all knowledge is precious even if not of the slightest human use'. I am certainly of this opinion and still hold to the basic principles underlying this thought. Schools need to teach us both about the past and about our futures. Let's look at what they should teach.

Immediately presents a reflective and sophisticated overview that focuses on the key question considered

Maintains personal engagement with the topic

Audience interest is maintained by sophisticated use of syntax and resulting balance

Includes relevant quotations from research

Vocabulary continues to be of high standard with low-frequency words used accurately and effectively

So far, the content is full, eloquent and very well organised with every reason to believe this standard will be maintained and further developed. This is a very different viewpoint and approach from Rebekah's but equally valid and clearly sustained at a high level mmediately on task

Very sweeping assertion with no supporting evidence

A series of personal complaints rather than a reflective overview of all the key issues

Meliz

I am going to talk about schools of the future. I don't think schools today do anything to prepare students for the world of the future. Most of them don't teach you anything useful in life and are just annoying. I don't know anyone who thinks schools teach you want you need to know. I don't know anyone who likes studying algebra. It's just stupid. You have to do equations in class all the time and it's boring. In English you read too many books and in science there are lots of pointless practicals. I'd rather learn a lot more coding to help me with my gaming. This isn't an education to prepare us for the future. We will make lots of money from the skills we learn in gaming and we get all our interaction on social media. What's the point of school? The world's not going to end without it!

Gives a clear perspective but expressed in functional language rather than in a more mature style

Repetitive, and vocabulary lacks sophistication

Another rant so the content continues to be thin and uninspiring

Immediately on task, reflective and offering a valid perspective in a considered tone

A measured, planned and organised reply which considers the wider perspective and maintains personal engagement in a reflective way

Rebekah

I understand the need for schools and I know we can't be without them but I have to say life at school can be really frustrating. In my talk I'm going to cover some of the ways schools of the future will change and other things which will stay the same and keep what is useful about school. I'm going to offer some alternative ways of learning like MOOCs and online interaction, as the whole idea of schools and classrooms – and especially exams – is flawed. Together, students, parents and teachers can work to make schools into places that are not stuck in the past but really try to prepare us for the future world.

I'd like to start with the school day and curriculum. Why start the day so early? And why cover subjects that are all about the past instead of the future? We should keep our focus on science and technology to prepare us for a world of constant change.

Clearly sets out aims of the talk and offers a balanced view

Vocabulary is used soundly and syntax is sufficiently mature to allow the talk to flow, so audience interest is being maintained

Level of vocabulary is appropriate (more than merely functional) without being particularly sophisticated

Tip

You will be assessed on the organisation of your content in addition to the viewpoint you adopt. Don't worry about trying to give a 'right' answer. You should express your opinions, with appropriate support from your research, and always show a sense of awareness of your listener or audience.

Enable

At the beginning of this Assessment workshop, one of your targets was to deliver a spoken presentation promoting your own viewpoint with confidence.

Read the following short speech out loud.

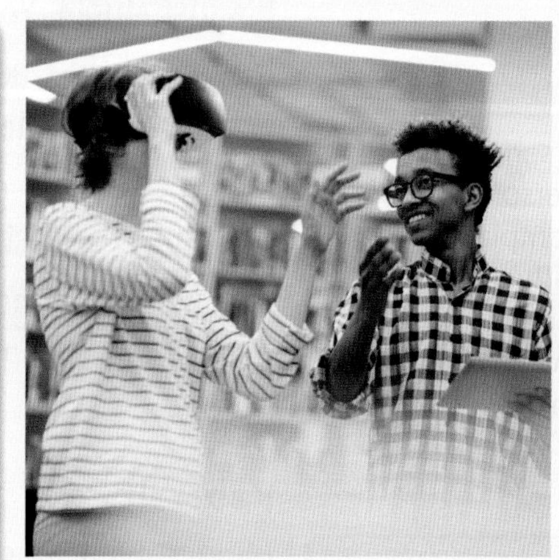

What will future learning in schools and colleges be like?

Technology is moving quickly and the pace of change towards a virtual world has been accelerated by the 2020 global pandemic. Classrooms could be obsolete. The classroom of the future will become a virtual experience and the teacher will facilitate very different learning models which are much more tailored to the individual student.

Will schools become part-time? Blended learning and the flipped classroom mean that the student will do lots of what they used to do in school but at home, or remotely. Home will become the best place to learn facts and ideas. Well, not just home, but any working space that has connectivity. However, the classroom will surely remain essential as the hub of teaching and learning. It will always be the place for interaction with other students.

But what will a learning centre of the future look like? Comfortable pods where students interact with tablets, virtual reality equipment as the norm. And will an extra-curricular programme be even more important as an alternative to spending hours and days on screen? Could extra-curricular activities also go online?

Intelligent robots might replace teachers for many tasks as they can be programmed to deliver learning exactly to fit the level of each learner. How excellent is that! The teacher will be first and foremost a facilitator – an assistant in this new learning process. Pastoral skills are likely to be more important than subject knowledge. Teachers might still work with groups, however, to develop communication and collaboration skills; perhaps in ever-blended models of learning.

New methods of assessment and exams will be needed. Maybe in the future schools will not need exams as all learning will be based on an individual's aims and objectives. We can say goodbye to those grades!

Follow up – recording a sustained talk

Respond to the following task.

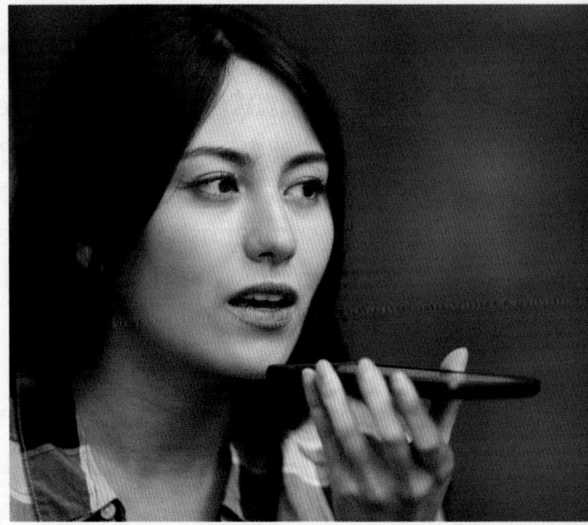

Prepare and record a five-minute talk of your own with the same topic:

'What will future learning in schools and colleges be like?'

You should make some different points and extend these with examples. In a five-minute talk, you also have time to include a short anecdote.

You may wish to consider:

- ways you have seen teaching and learning change in your time at school or college
- science and technology advances that will shape future teaching and learning
- how people are prepared for the big changes to future work and employment
- whether some countries are able to keep up with others in optimising technology for teaching and learning
- how students will need to adapt their learning styles and lifestyle for the new ways of learning

Tip

The prompts you are given increase in difficulty so you can show your speaking skills to best advantage. Start by giving easier, concrete examples to build your confidence. Finish your talk by dealing with some more sophisticated, abstract ideas.

When you have finished, discuss your recorded talk with your teacher.

7 Focus on William Blake

In this unit, you will engage with how some poets, including the world-renowned Romantic poet William Blake, have chosen to represent members of the animal world. You will read about interactions with snakes, a frightening confrontation with an apex predator and how a species of shark relies on a much smaller fish to survive. You will listen to a fascinating discussion between two students on how a famous poem should be interpreted. You will also practise constructing a persuasive argument successfully.

And in doing all that, you will be practising these key skills:

Speaking & Listening

- Collaborate successfully within a group to create a poem about an animal predator.
- Reflect on the effect that different performances of the same oral piece can have on listeners.

Writing

- Create an effective personal opinion piece regarding the importance of a selection of poetry.
- Use effective punctuation to create complex sentences relating to the life and works of William Blake.

Reading

- Extract significant meaning from texts that are written using sustained imagery.
- Analyse the effect of rhythm, intonation and emphasis when interpreting a poem.

Assessment workshop

You will gain practice in the key assessment skill of responding to a non-fiction text and analysing its viewpoint. You will respond effectively to questions requiring both short and extended answers regarding the effect of viewpoint in a persuasive text.

Thinking time

1. Think of as many ways as possible in which a poem differs from a story. Is there anything a poem can do better?
2. Can poets write about subjects like cheese, or should poetry be about things like flowers, rivers and mountains? Can you think of an unusual subject for a poem?
3. What does Salman Rushdie mean by all of the items he lists in a poet's work?

"Poetry is a mirror that makes beautiful that which is distorted."
Percy Bysshe Shelley

"A poet's work is to name the unnameable, to point out frauds, to take sides, start arguments, shape the world, and stop it going to sleep."
Salman Rushdie

"The poets have been mysteriously silent on the subject of cheese."
G.K. Chesterton

Speaking & Listening – predator poetry game

A predator hunts or preys on other creatures. Here are some examples: hyena, wild boar, crocodile, leopard, king cobra, piranha fish, grizzly bear, grey wolf, shark, komodo dragon.

Begin by finding out some facts about these animals. Make notes that you could use.

The game is to make up a poem, with someone writing it down.

- Choose a predator. Decide how many lines to have in your poem. You may change your mind, particularly if the poem works well and you want to go on.
- The leader starts with a single line of five words, like 'I am a king cobra'.
- The next person adds a line of five words, perhaps ending with a word that rhymes or a word that would be easy to rhyme with.
- Carry on round the group, each person adding a line of five words.
- When you want to end the poem, make a line that everyone can shout together.
- Perform your poem.

You may want to use several lines to describe your animal: its eyes, its teeth, the sounds it makes, how it moves and, in general, how frightening it is. That could help you with your last line.

Remember the golden rule – choose your words to make the best effect. You can add alliteration, onomatopoeia, similes and metaphors.

The snake experience

Discuss what you would write about if you had to write a poem about a snake. What do you think about immediately someone says "Snake!" to you?

Now decide how you want to read these two poems aloud. Remember not to pause until you come to a punctuation mark, or you might lose the meaning.

Snake (excerpt)

A snake came to my water-trough
On a hot, hot day, and I in pyjamas for the heat,
To drink there.

In the deep, strange-scented shade of the great dark carob tree
I came down the steps with my pitcher
And must wait, must stand and wait, for there he was at the trough
before me.
He reached down from a fissure in the earth-wall in the gloom
And trailed his yellow-brown slackness soft-bellied down, over
the edge of the stone trough
And rested his throat upon the stone bottom,
And where the water had dripped from the tap, in a small clearness,
He sipped with his straight mouth,
Softly drank through his straight gums, into his slack long body,
Silently.

Someone was before me at my water-trough,
And I, like a second-comer, waiting.

He lifted his head from his drinking, as cattle do,
And looked at me vaguely, as drinking cattle do,
And flickered his two-forked tongue from his lips, and mused
a moment,
And stooped and drank a little more,
Being earth-brown, earth-golden from the burning bowels
of the earth
On the day of Sicilian July, with Etna smoking.

The voice of my education said to me
He must be killed,
For in Sicily the black, black snakes are innocent, the gold
are venomous.

And voices in me said, If you were a man
You would take a stick and break him now, and finish him off.

D. H. Lawrence

Glossary

Etna a volcano in southern Italy that is constantly active, hence 'smoking'

fissure a long and narrow opening in a rock made by cracking or splitting

pitcher a large potter jug usually used to hold water

To the snake

Green Snake, when I hung you round my neck
and stroked your cold, **pulsing** throat
as you hissed to me, glinting
arrowy gold scales, and I felt
the weight of you on my shoulders,
and the whispering silver of your dryness
sounded close at my ears –

Green Snake – I swore to my companions that certainly
you were harmless! But truly
I had no certainty, and no hope, only desiring
to hold you, for that joy,
which left
a long wake of pleasure, as the leaves moved
and you faded into the pattern
of grass and shadows, and I returned
smiling and haunted, to a dark morning.

Denise Levertov

Word cloud

arrowy	**wake**
pulsing	**whispering**

Understanding

1. What is the most obvious difference between the two snakes?
2. Explain what is happening in each poem and in what sense they are reflective (that is, how they represent the writers' thoughts).
3. Discuss how each writer addresses the snake, the first calling it 'he' and the second 'you'. Why is it important to the poems that the snakes are not addressed as 'it'?
4. Titles are important when you write a poem (or a story). Discuss what you think of the titles of these two poems.
5. Do you think the poet was reckless to pick up the green snake without knowing if it was venomous or not? Why?
6. Imagine you are the gardener in the poem 'Snake'. Write what you would say about the events that make up the poem as if you are talking to some friends.

Remember

Poems often contain plenty of imagery . In 'To the snake', you will notice that imagery is used because the writer wants us to feel exactly what she experienced when she picked up the snake. Imagery should be used for a purpose.

Word builder

Poets often use regular words to convey a different meaning. In poetry the use of words is more flexible and we often see unusual combinations of words in phrases to add to the poem's effect.

Answer these questions about the unusual use of words by the writer of 'To the snake'.

1. Why is 'arrowy gold scales' better than *pointed*?
2. Why is 'cold, pulsing throat' better than *moving*?
3. How does the use of 'whispering silver of your dryness' create a better effect than using *mumbling*?
4. The word wake is a noun that is usually associated with somebody who has died. How then can this experience be a 'wake of pleasure'?

Global Perspectives

Snake bites and injuries from similar predators cause death to humans in many parts of the world, yet most of these animals will try to avoid confrontation. How much of an issue is this in your region? Research to find out how this compares with other countries where predators dangerous to humans are prevalent. In what ways can authorities more successfully educate people to avoid such dangers?

Developing your language – writing about an encounter with a snake

To describe something really well you first need to think of your own Word cloud. Here are some more snake words that you might be able to find.

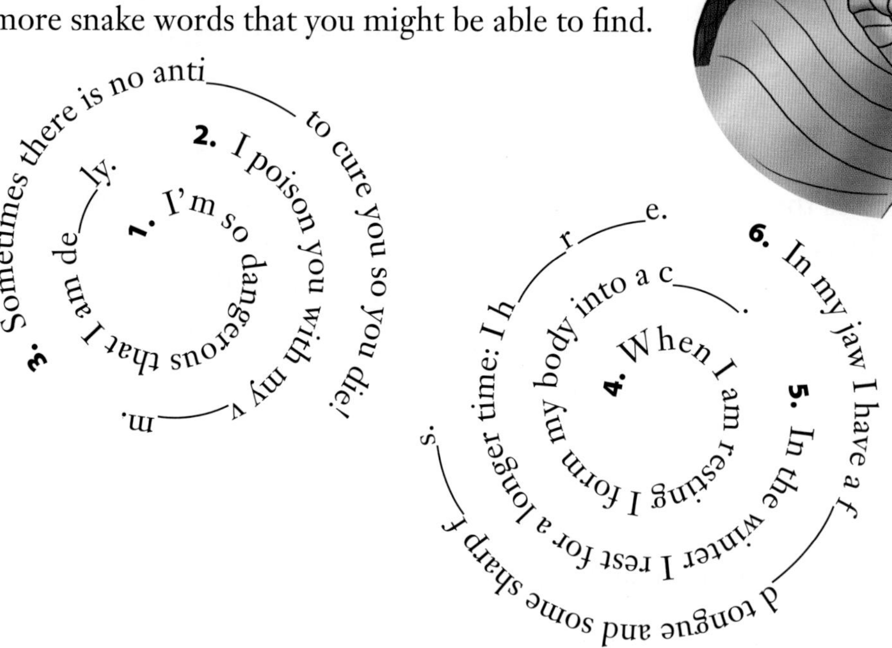

Imagine you suddenly discover a snake. Write two paragraphs. In the first, describe what you see and hear and, in the second, what happens. Remember to include your feelings at the time and afterwards.

Developing your language – writing from notes

Here are some notes made from researching snakes. The notes are in the note-maker's own words and are not copied from the source. They are in no particular order.

1 Long, no legs, eat animals (no veg), are reptiles
2 Use smell to find prey – forked tongue collects particles
3 In all continents except Antarctica (not Ireland or New Zealand)
4 20 families – length varies from 10cm to nearly 7 metres
5 Most non-poisonous – rare human deaths, but some amputation
6 Find prey by sensing vibrations in the ground
7 Usually avoid humans – venom used for catching prey and digesting it, not self-defence
8 Skin scaly – NOT slimy! (people think it is)
9 Some live in sea (Indian and Pacific Oceans)
10 Skulls have joints so can swallow prey bigger than head
11 Prey – lizard, frog, bird, egg, fish, snail

Imagine someone has set up a website about predators and has asked you to write a short entry on the topic of snakes. It has to be factual, not a story or a description. You have found all sorts of interesting facts which are listed above.

Use the facts to write your entry.

To help you:

- **Beginning and end:** Which items are best to start and to finish?
- **Get the best order:** For example, there are three notes about snakes' prey; these will have to go together.
- **Develop the wording of your notes:** For example, in item 8 you could write People often mistakenly think ....
- **Write your own words:** Develop your own style, as in item 3: Snakes are found in nearly every corner of the world....

Remember

Never copy whole sentences and phrases from the Internet, encyclopedias or textbooks. Always try to develop your own style of writing.

'The Tyger' – a poem for discussion

Listen to the audio for this task:

Here are two students, Abellia and Rashid, talking about the first verse of a very famous poem. Their teacher has asked them to prepare a reading of the verse, but they have decided to begin by working out what the poet Willliam Blake is saying to them.

The whole poem is printed below. You will need it later for your own discussion and reading.

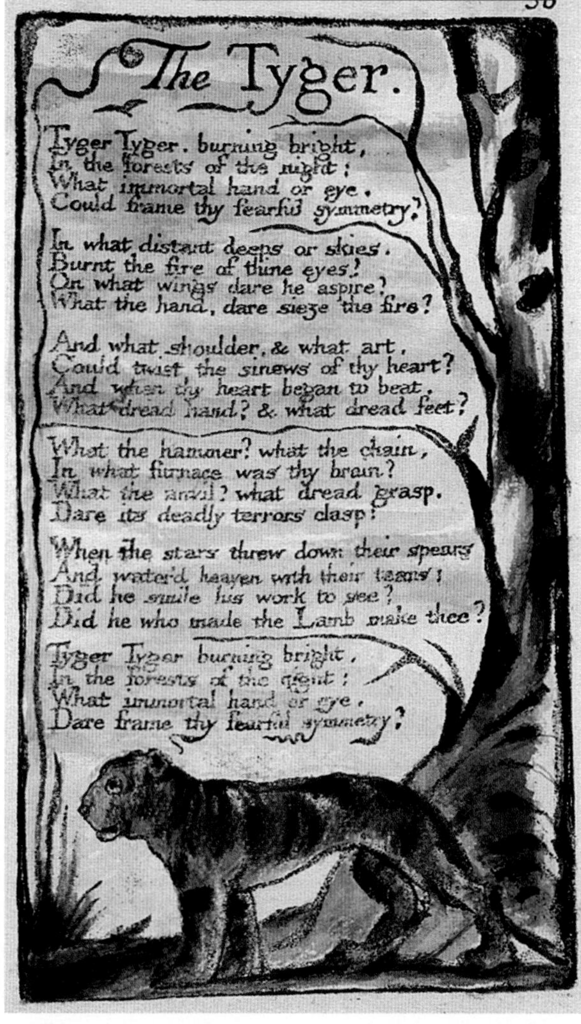

Understanding

1. Why did Abellia think that Rashid's first attempt at reading the verse was not good enough?
2. How do you know that William Blake meant his tiger to sound scary?
3. Blake said the tiger was 'burning bright', which makes him sound as if he were on fire. How did Rashid explain what Blake imagined?
4. What effect is created by the use of alliteration in the first verse?
5. Do you think this poem was written for children or adults? Explain what you think.
6. Imagine you are standing in a clearing in the jungle when you see the tiger approaching. What are your thoughts and how do you react?

The Tyger

Tyger Tyger, burning bright,
In the forests of the night;
What immortal hand or eye,
Could frame thy fearful symmetry?

In what distant deeps or skies,
Burnt the fire of thine eyes?
On what wings dare he aspire?
What the hand, dare seize the fire?

And what shoulder, what art,
Could twist the sinews of thy heart?
And when thy heart began to beat,
What dread hand? what dread feet?

What the hammer? what the chain,
In what furnace was thy brain?
What the anvil? what dread grasp,
Dare its deadly terrors clasp?

When the stars threw down their spears
And water'd heaven with their tears:
Did he smile his work to see?
Did he who made the Lamb make thee?

Tyger Tyger, burning bright,
In the forests of the night:
What immortal hand or eye,
Dare frame thy fearful symmetry?

William Blake

'The Lamb' – a poem for comparison

This is the first verse of a poem William Blake wrote in direct contrast to 'The Tyger'. The image of a tiger represents a dangerous predator but the image of a lamb represents innocence.

The Lamb

Little Lamb who made thee
Dost thou know who made thee
Gave thee life & bid thee feed.
By the stream & o'er the mead;
Gave thee clothing of delight,
Softest clothing wooly bright;
Gave thee such a tender voice,
Making all the vales rejoice!
Little Lamb who made thee
Dost thou know who made thee

William Blake

1. Copy and complete the table to show how Blake builds a picture of innocence in 'The Lamb'. The first quotation has been identified for you.

Image intended	Quotation
Small and vulnerable	'Little Lamb'
At one with the peaceful landscape	
Innocent appearance	
Peaceful soft sound	
Welcomed in the environment	

2. Re-read 'The Tyger'. Organise the words and phrases in the box (right) into conflicting pairs. Then match each word or phrase to either 'The Tyger' or 'The Lamb' to complete your comparison. The first pair is identified for you.

'The Tyger'	'The Lamb'
Intimidating appearance	Unthreatening

Glossary

mead meadow

o'er short for *over*

vales valleys

unthreatening dark
contentment silent
night fear
light day
prey predator
intimidating appearance
simple language used
violent imagery
peaceful imagery
complex vocabulary
gentle sound

Punctuation – punctuating complex sentences

Proofread the paragraph and add the necessary punctuation, including commas and full stops.

To help you, these are the conjunctions that are used in the paragraph: *and*, *because*, *so*, *when*, *who*, *which*.

Blake first name William was born in 1757 he died in 1827 like many other artists Blake was not considered important during his lifetime in fact he was something of an outsider because he did not come from a wealthy family most poets of the time were independently wealthy which meant they could pursue their dreams being a poet did not pay well so Blake trained as an engraver many of his poems were accompanied by engravings when he published them living in London during the Industrial Revolution a time of great social change inspired much of Blake's writing he witnessed the pain that poverty caused to those in need who the rich and powerful ignored deeply affected and concerned Blake wrote of a more innocent age when humans were more in tune with nature.

Abellia and Rashid are discussing the use of conjunctions:

Rashid: So I can't join sentences with *this*, *I*, *he*, *she*, *it* or *they*?

Abellia: No, none of those because they are pronouns and not conjunctions. You can't use *then* either. Look, I'll show you: 'Blake is a great poet. His imagery is so beautiful I cannot stop thinking about it.'

Rashid: I see. So it's a full stop after 'William' and not a comma.

1. On the next page is an extract from a piece of fictional writing composed by Abellia called 'I'd rather be a tiger than a lamb'. Explain why the commas have been used.

Remember

Subordinate clauses are unable to stand alone as a complete sentence. They are also sometimes called dependent clauses. More words are required therefore to make a sentence. For example, 'because he did not come from a wealthy family' is subordinate as the sentence it might feature in will complete the required detail.

If I had to choose between being a tiger or a lamb, I couldn't get Blake's poems out of my mind when I went to sleep last night, I would certainly choose the former. Tigers are fierce, independent, and so regal, unlike meek little lambs. They roam around their territory knowing that they are the apex predator, completely unafraid of any other animal. All lambs do is eat grass, stand in a field all day, and wait to be told what to do by some grumpy sheepdog. What kind of existence is that? Yes, I would definitely choose to be a tiger if my strange dream comes true!

Abellia says: "I put a full stop after 'choose the former' in line 3 because the next sentence begins with 'Tigers', which isn't a conjunction. I put commas around 'I couldn't get Blake's poems out of my mind when I went to sleep last night' because it is extra information that interrupts the flow of the first sentence. If it was removed, the first sentence would still be complete."

2. Rashid is proofreading the following paragraph and he has found some mistakes.

I have to admit that I find lambs adorable they are so full of life. They make such wonderful little bleating sounds, they just make you want to pick them up and cuddle them. It seems that they have no cares in the world, they just run around playing with other lambs until they are tired. The most impressive feature of a lamb is its sad eyes, they make you melt and seem to say: 'I know I'm very cute so please feed me some delicious milk'.

Rashid says: "Put a full stop after 'adorable' because 'they' is a pronoun, not a conjunction. Better still, join the two sentences together by writing 'I have to admit that I find lambs adorable because they are so full of life'. 'Because' is a conjunction."

3. Find three other wrongly punctuated pairs of sentences in the paragraph. Say why the commas are wrong and use conjunctions to join each pair together.

   Decide whether you need extra commas. Sometimes you should split up a complicated sentence, but often a comma disturbs the flow.

A predator of the sea

The Maldive Shark

About the Shark, phlegmatical one,
Pale sot of the Maldive sea,
The sleek little pilot-fish, azure and slim,
How alert in attendance be.
From his **saw-pit** of mouth, from his **charnel** of maw
They have nothing of harm to dread,
But liquidly glide on his **ghastly** flank
Or before his Gorgonian head;
Or lurk in the port of **serrated** teeth
In white triple **tiers** of glittering gates,
And there find a haven when peril's abroad,
An asylum in jaws of the Fates!
They are friends; and friendly they guide him to prey,
Yet never partake of the treat—
Eyes and brains to the dotard lethargic and dull,
Pale **ravener** of horrible meat.

Herman Melville

Word cloud

charnel	saw-pit
ghastly	serrated
ravener	tiers

Understanding

1. What does the poem tell you about the pilot fish?
2. Why is the pilot fish a friend of the shark?
3. In what ways does the writer portray the shark?
4. How does the poet show the difference in intelligence between the shark and the pilot fish?
5. What makes you think that the writer had experience of the sea? Does this make the poem better? Why?
6. Imagine that you see a Maldive shark at close quarters. Write a diary account of what you saw.

Glossary

dotard silly old person

Gorgonian petrifying because, in myths, you turned to stone if you looked at a Gorgon

maw stomach of a hungry animal

phlegmatical not easily excited or worried

sot idiot

Word builder

Pay close attention to the vocabulary of the poem because it gives an accurate picture of sea life. The words in the Word cloud, in particular, give us a very real picture of the shark.

1. Why does Melville use the word *tiers* for the shark's teeth?
2. A long time ago, people used to confuse the word *ghastly* with *ghostly*. What do you imagine when you see the word *ghastly*? The word *aghast* means terrified, so how does this word make you feel about the shark?
3. *Ravenous* means eating hungrily, with the idea of tearing your meal apart. How does Melville's word 'ravener' add to what you feel about this shark?
4. You know about the danger of sharks to humans when they bite. How does *serrated* explain why a shark attack is so terrible?
5. Why does Melville use *charnel* to describe the shark's stomach? Charnels are usually found in burial grounds, not inside animals.
6. What does the image of a saw-pit suggest about the size of the shark's mouth and teeth?

Developing your language – poetic imagery

1. Use the words of the poem to discuss why this cartoon of a shark isn't like the one you have read about. List the ways in which it is different.
2. Draw your own cartoon of the Maldive shark. You can draw it from any angle or distance.
3. Look further at the words Melville uses to describe the shark's teeth:

   'Or lurk in the port of serrated teeth

   In white triple tiers of glittering gates'

   Why does he describe them as white, glittering gates and in what way are they a port? How does *haven* suggest the same thing?
4. Look at the way the pilot fish are described:

   'The sleek little pilot-fish, azure and slim… liquidly glide.'

   Why are they called pilot fish? What do 'sleek', 'azure', slim', 'liquidly' and 'glide' add to the picture of the fish?
5. Now you have had a chance to study the poem, what do you think of it? Write a paragraph saying why you do or don't enjoy it.

Global Perspectives

Certain species of sharks and tigers are some of the most endangered animals on the planet. They are still hunted for their organs and as trophies. Those who benefit from this type of hunting and the trading of endangered species often do so illegally. Is this a problem in your local or regional area? How might you contribute to communicating the problems of this global issue and, hopefully, to eradicating it?

Expressing preferences and opinions

You must be responsible for any preference or opinion you express in either oral or written form if your ideas are to be listened to and given credit. Good writers sometimes offer very strong opinions but do so in a sensitive way that invites dialogue and discussion not uncontrolled argument and insult.

1. Explain why these opinions are not expressed in a sensitive way.

- **a** 'I hate this poem – it's boring!!!'
- **b** 'Why write a poem about a snake? Snakes are horrible and everyone hates them anyway.'
- **c** 'I don't like Blake's poems though I've never read any of them.'
- **d** 'Don't get me started on people who quote lines from poetry all the time – they're so irritating!'

2. Write four sentences starting with these words:

- **a** In my opinion …
- **b** I think that …
- **c** For me, there are advantages and disadvantages about …
- **d** On reflection I can see your point but have to say that …

Remember

It is just as important to provide evidence for an opinion as it is for a fact.

3. On first reading, 'The Lamb' by William Blake appears to be very simple and almost childish in its use of structure and vocabulary. In actual fact, the poem is much more complex, representing innocence and freedom.

Write a short paragraph of three to four sentences in which you reply to a fellow student who thinks 'The Lamb' is too simple to be considered an important poem.

Here are some ideas to start your sentences but use your own words if you wish to.

I accept that the structure of 'The Lamb' seems simple but …

The language used in the poem is deliberately plain because …

'The Tyger' uses more complex imagery because it represents experience whereas 'The Lamb' …

Even the landscape seems childlike in 'The Lamb'. However, it reflects …

Structuring your opinions

Poetry seems to divide opinion much more than any other genre. Two students can study the same poem and think its meaning is entirely different. Perhaps this is because a poem requires more personal interpretation from the reader than a story or a play.

Imagine that a competition for best poem has resulted in four finalists: 'To the snake', 'Medallion', 'The Tyger' and 'The Maldive Shark'. You have been asked to judge the winner.

You are going to present a short speech explaining your choice at the awards evening.

Write a plan for the speech to justify your decision. Include your reasons for putting your chosen poem in first place. Remember that your intention is not to upset any of the entrants so your opinions should be expressed sensitively.

WB Test the skills you have used in this unit on page 66 of the Workbook.

How you might structure your speech

Speech writers often plan their speeches in sections using cue cards. They write notes, which do not have to be in full sentences but should make sense and act as prompts that quickly remind the writer of all they want to say.

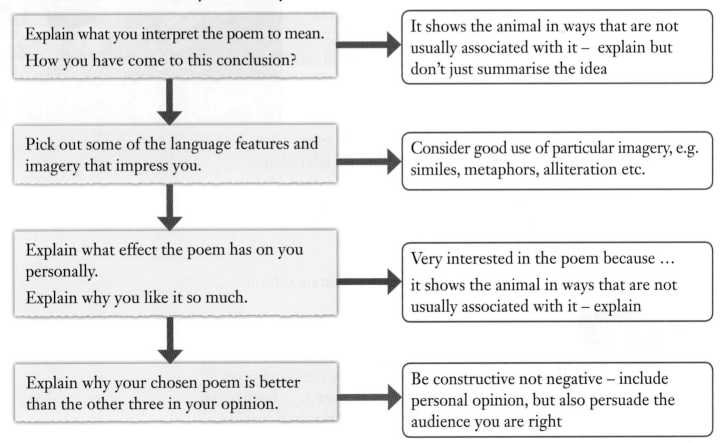

Explain what you interpret the poem to mean.
How you have come to this conclusion?
→ It shows the animal in ways that are not usually associated with it – explain but don't just summarise the idea

↓

Pick out some of the language features and imagery that impress you.
→ Consider good use of particular imagery, e.g. similes, metaphors, alliteration etc.

↓

Explain what effect the poem has on you personally.
Explain why you like it so much.
→ Very interested in the poem because …
it shows the animal in ways that are not usually associated with it – explain

↓

Explain why your chosen poem is better than the other three in your opinion.
→ Be constructive not negative – include personal opinion, but also persuade the audience you are right

Establish

After you complete this section, you will be able to:

- ➔ identify a writer's viewpoint and bias
- ➔ understand how a writer can manipulate a viewpoint and its effect on the reader
- ➔ structure a successful response to a non-fiction text, using appropriate persuasive features and different written formats.

If a text is written to persuade the reader to agree with a certain viewpoint, the writer's bias will be present. Bias may be very subtle but sometimes it is not, as in the text below. Often, such a text will be written to deliberately cause a reaction from the reader, who may strongly agree or disagree with the views expressed.

Read this text carefully and think about the writer's opinions about the conservation of tigers.

Don't save the tigers

There's a lot of nonsense talked about spending a lot of money to make sure tigers do not become extinct. After all, animals do become extinct every now and again. It is part of a natural process after all and tigers are no exception. You can spend a whole lot of money that could be spent on world poverty for example, in protecting these animals which let's face it, cause a good deal of pain to villagers in areas where they live. How would you like your animals killed and even your friends and relatives? It's not as if many of you will ever see a tiger in the wild. There are plenty of films on television and cameras can get close up, closer than you would dare. If you really want to see these smelly animals live, then go to a zoo. That's just as good. Seeing a tiger is no great deal; they are just a big cat, and there are plenty of those about.

Vikram Ghosh

Engage

Complete the following two tasks to draw out the writer's opinions and find counter-arguments to them. You will then engage further by writing a letter arguing that the tiger should be a protected species.

1. Start to gather the writer's opinions. Two opinions have been provided for you and you can complete the others.
   - **a** Extinction is part of the natural process.
   - **b** You could spend the money put aside for conservation on better things.
   - **c** Tigers can kill ____________________
   - **d** Few of you will ever see ____________________
   - **e** You get closer to a tiger by watching ____________________
   - **f** If you must see them live, go ____________________
   - **g** Tigers are nothing more than ____________________
2. Write a list of seven counter-arguments to the seven opinions listed above.

   The first one is completed for you as an example.
   - **a** Extinction is often caused by human interference in the natural world.

Tip

Understanding the writer's viewpoint is a key element of successfully responding to a text.

Being able to identify bias allows you to interpret the writer's intention so you can take it into account in your own response to the text.

Engaging with viewpoint

Write a letter to Vikram Ghosh arguing that tigers should be protected and disagreeing with his views.

In your letter, comment on what the writer says and argue against him. Decide which of his views you disagree with most, and explain why. Don't write about the topic, just his views.

Structure your letter into three paragraphs, following the advice below. You do not need to respond to all Ghosh's views.

Your first paragraph is an introduction. It gives your reaction to the text as a whole and makes your position clear. This is how you might begin:

Dear Vikram Ghosh

I recently read an article you wrote about the conservation of tigers. I think that the tiger is a specially beautiful animal and an important part of the food chain, and I would be very sad if this important species were to die out...

You could go on to quote what Ghosh says.

In your article you say 'It is part of a natural process after all and tigers are no exception.' I agree that extinction is often a part of a natural process, but in this case it is different because...

Or you could start a paragraph by saying:

My chief reason for disagreeing with you is...

You could begin your final paragraph:

To sum up my objections to your article...

Tip

It is important to include your own comments and opinions but make sure they are all directly relevant to the points made by the writer in the text you are responding to.

Evaluate

Carefully read these three answers to Vikram Ghosh's article and consider the strengths and weaknesses of each one.

Tip

It is never a good idea to respond to a non-fiction text in an informal style unless you are specifically asked to do so. Generally, use a formal style and standard English when answering questions in an exam.

Letter 1

Dear Vikram Ghosh

I read your silly article. I think you're talking a lot of tosh. What do you mean how would you like your friends and relatives killed? Serve them right for living near the tigers. What do they expect?

And another thing I didn't like it when you said about television. My TV hasn't got good reception so I can't see the programmes clearly, so what's the point of that?

I also read that tigers were smelly animals but I don't agree. They are big cats, so they spend a lot of time keeping clean.

I bet you don't really know much about tigers so what you say is silly.

Absit

Letter 2

Dear Vikram Ghosh

I read your article about conservation of tigers and, while I could understand your reasons, I thought the whole thing was very biased. In our modern global village, we know when an important species is in danger of extinction and we can do something about it, so extinction is not necessarily 'the natural order of things'. I find this argument illogical, yet it is fundamental to your whole article.

You say that 'not many of you will see a tiger in the wild'. That is true, but it is not a point against conservation. The tiger holds a vital place in the hierarchy of animals, and the food chain. It is just as illogical to compare spending money on conservation with relieving world poverty. They are different things and have no relation to each other.

The thought of seeing tigers in zoos does not appeal to me. I am sure that tigers in the wild are not smelly. Cages or muddy enclosures are not good environments for these noble animals. No wonder they look tired and are smelly.

You take the easy way out. I would rather work to guarantee the tiger's safety.

Yours sincerely

Anita Allee

Letter 3

Dear Vikram Ghosh

Did you know that poachers are killing tigers as I write and that you can contribute to a fund to adopt a tiger? If you did you would feel closer to the tiger population even if you never saw a wild one.

I don't accept your idea about tigers being 'just a big cat'. Have you ever looked closely at a tiger's face and seen those lovely colours? No cat's like that.

I half agree with your opinion about watching tigers on TV. With a big screen it is exciting. However, it would be better in proper 3D so that tigers could leap at you. Anyway, producers decide what you see.

Then there is your point about spending a lot of money. We don't actually spend much on tigers and we spend far more on world poverty.

Perhaps we should spend some money helping poor villagers whose animals and relatives get attacked by tigers. I see your point, but it doesn't happen to most of us, probably just in India, so that isn't a reason for letting them get extinct.

Yours sincerely

Alfredo

1. Put the three answers in order: best, less good and least good. How did you decide on the order?
2. Which answer shows the best understanding of the article?
3. Which reasons in each answer are good and which are less good?
4. There are no errors in the writing, but which is written in the best language and the best order?
5. How does your own letter compare to the three examples? What improvements could you make based on what you have learned?

Tip

Pay close attention to who is the intended audience for your writing.

In an exam, the ultimate audience is the examiner, who can only award marks based on what you have actually written.

Bear both audiences in mind. For example, you may be writing an article for a teenage blog, but the examiner will expect standard English, unless you are using informal language for a specific reason, such as speech.

Enable

At the beginning of this Assessment workshop, one of your targets was to understand how a writer can manipulate a viewpoint and its effects on the reader.

Read the extract about tigers on the next page. The writer describes the conflicting feelings awakened by a visit to a local zoo.

Predator or prey?

When I was a child, I loved to visit zoos, safari parks, aquariums; indeed anything remotely connected to the animal world. I was fascinated by being so close to actual animals that I had only previously experienced second-hand through the lens of someone else's camera. I soaked up every live image laid before me be it mammal, reptile, amphibian, or fish. It didn't matter to this prepubescent human sponge. Yet, even then, there was one animal that stood out, that commanded my attention above all others. The tiger!

Whenever I received that most glorious of opportunities to visit the tiger enclosure at my local zoo, I would pester my parents to the point of insanity to stay just that little while longer, to stare in awe at that perfect symmetry so vividly described by Blake.

Then came the teenage years and with them a growing awareness that encountering such magnificence through the bars of a cage was an exercise in cruelty that became increasingly difficult to justify. It gnawed at my conscience like a dog at a particularly tough table leg until I could no longer enjoy the experience without a sense of overriding guilt.

As a consequence, I had not visited a zoo since I was sixteen, some two decades ago, when I swore an oath to all animal kind to be a better person. That is until last week when finally I relented to the constant nagging of my own prepubescent sponges and took my two young daughters on a day out that they were anticipating as much as I was dreading.

And so, I found myself once again staring through the now detestable bars at those most noble of beasts, Sumatran tigers. And something strange happened to me, a paradox of desire to stay just a little while longer in the presence of such wonders of the natural world yet being totally reviled by their captivity. To be mere metres away from an apex predator was exhilarating and I was forced back to a time when my innocence prevailed yet the adult me stood horrified at the way these most terrifying of beasts had become a sideshow in humanity's desire for entertainment. From predator to prey.

I reluctantly drew myself away from the enclosure suffering a deep depression I still cannot overcome.

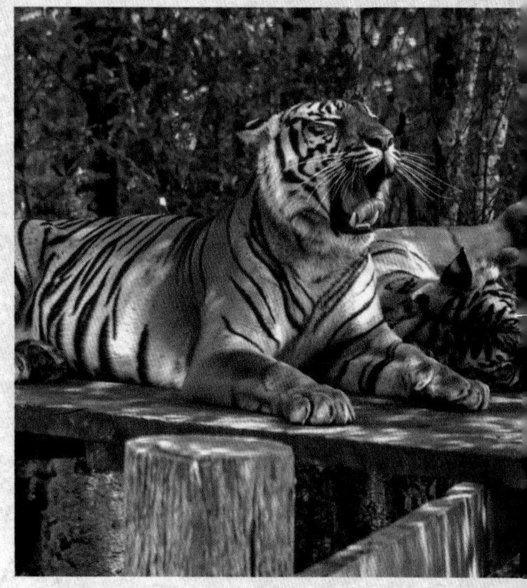

Glossary

apex predator top animal in its food chain

gnawed chewed

paradox contradiction (of ideas)

prepubescent at a young age before maturity

Tip

In trying to persuade, writers often use anecdotes to create an emotional response in the reader. Here the anecdote is about a childhood visit to see the tigers. It is important to identify anecdotes in a text and their purpose.

Consider the answers (in the box on the right) to these questions about how viewpoint is created in a non-fiction text. They will help you with the Follow-up task.

1. How does the viewpoint change between the start and end of the extract?
2. What reason does the writer give for the changing viewpoint in the text? Tick (√) **one** box.

   His daughters persuade him. ☐

   He misses visiting the zoo. ☐

   He has matured and become more aware. ☐

   Tigers are no longer of interest to him. ☐
3. Persuasive texts often use emotive language to emphasise important viewpoints. How do 'detestable bars' and 'most noble of beasts' try to persuade the reader that zoos are cruel?
4. Explain why the simile 'it gnawed at my conscience like a dog at a particularly tough table leg' is a suitable image to describe feeling guilty.
5. The writer describes conflicting feelings about viewing the tigers as a paradox. In your own words explain this paradox.

Follow up – writing an article

Decide on your viewpoint about zoos and respond to this task.

Write an article for your local newspaper considering what impact the proposed opening of a new zoo will have on your local area.

Think about:

- the impact a new zoo will have on your local environment set against any boost it will bring to the economy
- whether it is right to hold animals in captivity set against possible conservation programmes
- whether zoos are a necessary evil or unnecessary in modern society.

Spend about 30 minutes writing, once you have decided on your plan.

When you have finished, discuss your article with your teacher.

1. At the start, as a child, the writer loves to visit zoos and see animals in captivity, seeing nothing wrong with the idea. At the end, the grown-up writer is torn between liking to see animals close up and being disturbed to see them behind bars.
2. He has matured and become more aware.
3. The word 'detestable' is very emotive and shows how strongly the writer feels about animals being caged in zoos. The phrase 'most noble of beasts' suggests that tigers should be above such treatment and are demeaned by being held captive.
4. The word 'gnawed' suggests constant chewing. The writer's love of zoos gnaws at his conscience just as a dog chews a bone.
5. The writer still loves to see tigers close up as he admires them but cannot reconcile this with the idea that it is morally wrong to cage animals.

Tip

Some pieces of persuasive writing present both sides of an argument, though unequally, and leave the reader to decide their own viewpoint while still trying to persuade them to agree with the writer.

8 Cultures and communities

In this unit, you will engage with communities in different cultures, some of which face great difficulties. You will read about the effects of drought on the island of Trinidad and how the people who live in the Gobi Desert flourish in such a harsh environment. You will listen to an interesting discussion featuring a group of students from different countries discussing what their lives are like. You will also practise writing how to successfully begin a story using characterisation.

And in doing all that, you will be practising these key skills:

Speaking & Listening

- Work successfully within a group to discuss important world issues such as poverty.
- Understand the roles that can be taken in a discussion about the importance of water to people in different parts of the world.

Writing

- Create an effective beginning to a fictional story using suitable vocabulary to establish characterisation.
- Use conjunctions to create compound sentences relating to life in the Gobi Desert.

Reading

- Understand a text that contains non-standard English vocabulary in an extract written from the viewpoint of a native of Trinidad.
- Analyse the effect of vocabulary used to establish a specific tone when describing living in one of the world's most harsh environments.

Assessment workshop

You will gain practice in the key assessment skills of responding to a narrative text and analysing its content. You will respond effectively with short answers to questions about a literary text.

Thinking time

1. Think about what you see in the two pictures. What would it be like to live in those places? Which would you prefer?
2. What did Mark Twain mean when he said that kindness was 'the language which the deaf can hear and the blind can see'? Why do you think kindness is important?
3. What does Maya Angelou mean by 'bigotry'? How far does what she says defeat bigotry?

> "Smile at strangers and you just might change a life."
> **Steve Maraboli**

> "Kindness is the language which the deaf can hear and the blind can see."
> **Mark Twain**

> "Perhaps travel cannot prevent bigotry, but by demonstrating that all peoples cry, laugh, eat, worry and die, it can introduce the idea that if we try to understand each other, we may even become friends."
> **Maya Angelou**

Speaking & Listening – a presentation

Prepare a presentation about the place where you live and the people that live with you. Think about the order of your presentation and use pictures.

Here are some ideas to get you started:

- Where do you live?
- What is your home like?
- Describe some family members.
- Describe the area around where you live.
- Do you like living there? Where would you prefer to live when you grow up?

You could use some notes, or just use keywords to remind you what to say next.

Look at your audience and don't forget to smile.

Let them ask questions at the end.

How may a presentation on your school be different? Explain your answer.

A drink of water

The time when the rains didn't come for three months and the sun was a yellow **furnace** in the sky was known as the Great Drought in Trinidad. It happened when everyone was expecting the sky to burst open with rain to fill the dry streams and water the **parched** earth.

But each day was the same; the sun rose early in a blue sky, and all day long the farmers lifted their eyes, wondering what had happened. (...) They rested on their hoes and forks and wrung perspiration from their clothes, seeing no hope in labour, terrified by the thought that if no rain fell soon they would lose their crops and livestock and face starvation and death.

In the tiny village of Las Lomas, out in his vegetable garden, Manko licked dry lips and passed a wet sleeve over his dripping face. Somewhere in the field a cow mooed mournfully, sniffing around for a bit of green in the **cracked** earth. The field was a **desolation** of drought. The trees were naked and barks peeled off trunks as if they were diseased. When the wind blew, it was heavy and unrelieving, as if the heat had taken all the spirit out of it. But Manko still opened his shirt and turned his chest to it when it passed.

He was a big man, grown brown and burnt from years of working on the land. His arms were bent and he had a crouching position even when he stood upright. When he laughed he showed more tobacco stain than teeth.

But Manko had not laughed for a long time. Bush fires had swept Las Lomas and left the garden plots **charred** and smoking. Cattle were dropping dead in the heat. There was scarcely any water in the village; the river was dry with **scummy** mud. But with patience one could collect a bucket of water. Boiled, with a little sugar to make it drinkable, it had to do.

Sometimes, when the children knew that someone had gone to the river for water, they hung about in the village main road waiting with bottles and calabash shells, and they fell upon the water-carrier as soon as he hove in sight.

'Boil the water first before drinking!' was the warning cry. But even so two children were dead and many more were on the sick list, their parents too poor to seek medical aid in the city twenty miles away.

Word cloud

charred	**furnace**
cracked	**parched**
desolation	**scummy**

Manko sat in the shade of a mango tree and tried to look on the bright side of things. Such a dry season meant that the land would be good for corn seeds when the rains came. He and his wife Rannie had been working hard and saving money in the hope of sending Sunny, their son, to college in the city.

Rannie told Manko: 'We poor, and we ain't have no education, but is all right, we go get old soon and dead, and what we have to think about is the boy. We must let him have plenty learning and come a big man in Trinidad.'

And Manko, proud of his son, used to boast in the evening, when the villagers got together to talk and smoke, that one day Sunny would be a lawyer or a doctor.

But optimism was difficult now. His livestock was dying out, and the market was glutted with yams. He had a great pile in the yard which he could not sell.

Manko took a look at his plot of land and shook his head. There was no sense in working any more today.

From *A Drink of Water* by Samuel Selvon

Glossary

and come a big man in Trinidad and become someone important in Trinidad

we ain't have no education we don't have any education

we go get old soon and dead we shall soon be old and we'll die

we poor we are poor

Remember

Although the grammar is incorrect, this is how Rannie speaks. In a story, it is better to write people's speech as they would talk so it is more realistic and believable.

Understanding

1. What did the people of Las Lomas do for a living?
2. Do droughts like this happen often in Trinidad? Explain your answer.
3. How does the description of the trees make it clear how unusually bad the drought is?
4. Explain how the villagers got their water and what they did with it.
5. How do you know that life in Las Lomas was always difficult?
6. At the end of the passage the writer says how the villagers used to get together in the evening to talk and smoke. Imagine that you are Manko, talking to other villagers. The drought is really serious. What would you talk about? In your conversation you could include:
   - the state of the ground and the cattle
   - the serious matter of the water supply
   - when the drought might end
   - what will happen when the drought ends
   - your hopes for your children.

Global Perspectives

After doing some research, how dependent do you think your region is on its agriculture and the food it produces? Is exporting local produce an important industry in your country or is the importation of foodstuffs from the global market more significant?

Word builder

When the writer tells you about the heat in the wind, he calls it 'heavy and unrelieving'. The use of 'heavy' doesn't mean that the wind is physically heavy; he is saying that when the wind blows, the heat seems to push downwards and you have to fight against it.

Look at the words in the Word cloud describing how the earth suffers under terrible heat.

Answer the following questions. In your answers, show how the context changes the meanings of words.

1. Why has the writer used the word 'furnace' as a metaphor for the sun?
2. How did the garden plots come to be 'charred'? Describe what you would see.
3. What does the writer mean when he talks about the 'cracked earth'?
4. How does 'parched' personify the earth?
5. The writer talks about 'a desolation of drought'. Why is this expression effective?
6. Why did the writer say 'scummy mud' and not 'dirty mud'? What effect does 'scummy' add?

Remember

The vocabulary around the particular word you are thinking about gives it context. The context often changes the meaning of the word in some way.

Developing your language – how writers present character

In the extract from *A Drink of Water* you have only read about one person – or character – called Manko.

You know what Manko looked like – he was big, brown and burnt, had bent arms and back, and his teeth were stained from smoking – but this is his appearance, not his character.

Someone's character is what they are like, for example, you can work out that Manko was hard-working.

He was also slightly superstitious, as he wondered what had happened to the rain god.

Answer these questions.

1. The words and phrases below describe different aspects of Manko's character. Find a quotation from the text which describes each characteristic in a different way.
   - **a** A devoted father
   - **b** Optimistic even when times were bad
   - **c** Sociable
   - **d** Defiant
   - **e** Liked to laugh a lot
2. Imagine you are Sunny, Manko's son. You have become a famous doctor and have been asked to write about your early life and what you owe to your father. Write a paragraph about your memories of Manko.

Remember

When you choose words from a text to describe someone's character the choice is yours, but you should always find a quotation that supports your answer. For example, you could choose any of the following details:

- what the writer tells you
- what the person does and says
- what other people say about him or her.

Life among the animals

The people of the Gobi Desert live in one of the most **inhospitable** places on earth. It is a harsh, rocky environment, and it is landlocked. Its **nomadic** inhabitants travel several times a year on camels in search of water. They are accompanied by the animals that they herd: oxen, sheep, and most valuable and beloved of all, their horses. When they arrive at a suitable location, they set up their gers or yurts which can be easily constructed and **dismantled.** These circular tents with their woollen coverings provide coolness in the summer and protection from the extreme cold of the desert winter when the temperature falls drastically to a piercing –40° C. In summer there is warmth and the herders make the most of the pastures, leaving their horses outside to **forage** for themselves.

Every member of a **herder's** family possesses their own horse – in fact the population is smaller than the number of horses. Mongolians **process** mares' milk into airag, the national beverage, although they mainly use horses for riding, at which they are extremely accomplished. They are famous for horse racing for they gallop with great velocity. Women also have extensive knowledge of **horsemanship**. They say, 'A Mongolian without a horse is like a bird without wings.'

So if you want to visit the Gobi Desert, and love horses, you will be welcomed with open arms. These people are known for their hospitality and a proverb says, 'Happy is the one who has guests; merry is the home that boasts a tethering rail with many visitors' horses.'

Word cloud

dismantled
forage
herder
horsemanship
inhospitable
nomadic
process

Glossary

airag a light drink made from mares' milk, slightly sour to the taste

gers, yurts a special type of tent

tethering rail a bar for tying your horse to

velocity speed in a certain direction

with open arms with great friendship; pleased to see you

Understanding

Answer these questions.

1. What do the inhabitants of the Gobi Desert do for a living?
2. How do they travel about?
3. Explain how the yurts protect the herders and their families from the weather.
4. In what way do the women seem to be equal to the men?
5. Explain the proverb, 'A Mongolian without a horse is like a bird without wings.'
6. How would you prepare for a trip to this community?

Developing your language – words about a lifestyle

Someone's way of life is their lifestyle. Manko's lifestyle was one of poverty and back-breaking hard work for little reward.

Each of the words in the Word cloud hints at something that Mongolian nomads spend their time doing – that helps make up their lifestyle.

'Dismantled' tells you that their homes are made to be taken apart. Although they are comfortable and made with strong circular wooden frames, this word reminds you that they do not stay in the same place for long.

Answer the following questions.

1. The people described in the extract are said to be 'herders' and to live a 'nomadic' life. Explain what this tells you about their lifestyle.
2. What hints do the words 'horsemanship' and 'forage' give you about the interests of these nomads?
3. What hint does 'process' give you about the herders' way of life?
4. How does the use of 'inhospitable' to describe the Gobi Desert emphasise the challenges faced by the people who live there?

Writing about your lifestyle

Write two paragraphs about your lifestyle – work and play. Use the following ideas.

Paragraph 1

- What I do that seems like work, such as chores around the house, a part-time job, homework
- Who I do that work with and why
- How much time I spend doing that work and whether I think it is worthwhile

Paragraph 2

- What I do for recreation and play
- My favourite activities
- Who I share my activities with
- Which is more important to me, work or play?

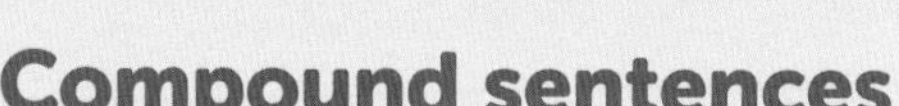

Compound sentences

You know about simple sentences, for example: *Every member of a herder's family possesses their own horse.*

You also know about coordinated sentences, for example: *It is a harsh, rocky environment, and it is landlocked.*

Discuss how this sentence is different.

When they arrive at a suitable location, they set up their gers or yurts which can be easily constructed and dismantled.

The main sentence (or clause) is: *They set up their gers or yurts.*

When they arrive at a suitable location tells you the time when they set up their tents.

Which can be easily constructed or dismantled tells you about the tents.

> **Remember**
>
> A simple sentence has one verb and one subject. Two sentences joined together by *and, but* or *so* are coordinated sentences.

1. **Answer the questions about this compound sentence:**

   Mongolians process mares' milk into airag, the national beverage, although they use horses mainly for riding, at which they are extremely accomplished.

   a How many verbs can you count in the compound sentence?

   b Which is the main clause and how do you know?

   c What word does 'at which' tell you about?

   d What do you think 'although' means?

2. **Which of these are main clauses and which are subordinate?**

   a You will be welcomed with open arms

   b That they herd

   c If you want to visit the Gobi Desert

   d The people of the Gobi Desert live in one of the most inhospitable places on earth

> **Remember**
>
> A main clause is the most important part of a compound sentence and is complete in itself. A subordinate clause tells you about a word in the main clause and does not make sense by itself.

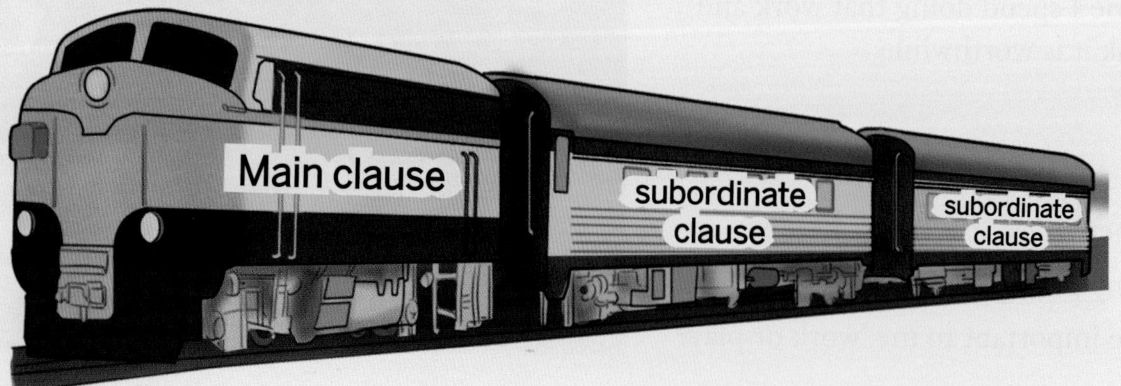

Conjunctions

Use the right conjunction for each gap. Then read the sentence to make sure it makes sense.

1. ________ I first read about the nomads of the Gobi Desert, they seemed to me to be tough people ________ they could survive such winter cold.
2. The nomads would not be able to survive ________ it was not for three things ________ are their tents, their animals and warm summers.
3. The Gobi Desert is an unusual place ________ I might like to go ________, of course, it was in mid-winter.

that	why	although	until	yet
after	while	when	how	where
which	because	as	if	before
who	since	for	unless	

Remember

Conjunctions are used to link sentences together. Examples: when, where, why, who, which, if, although, because, for, since, as, after, before, how, that, unless, until, while, yet.

Practice makes perfect

Use the conjunctions above to make some compound sentences of your own. Each one should have a main clause and two subordinate clauses – three verbs in all.

Danger ahead!

What is wrong with the following sentence? Explain your answer and write down an improved version.

I'm just back from Mongolia and I feel ill but I don't know why because I was careful what I had whenever it was mealtime when they gave you so much that I couldn't finish unless it was something I liked which wasn't often so they must've thought I was fussy but I'm not well because maybe it was something I ate, but I don't know.

Living in different countries

Listen to the audio for this task:

You are going to hear a group discussion about living in different countries. The teacher, Miss Favoro, has organised the discussion but does not take part. You will hear two girls, Sukhvinder and Melina, and two boys, Gopal and Angelo.

Before you listen, think about the contribution each student could make to the discussion. What could they think about the following statements?

1. Where you are born is just a matter of chance.
2. Water is important to everyone's lives.
3. Some people go to live in another country to look for a better life.

Understanding

1. What job did Miss Favoro give to Sukhvinder?
2. Why did she want Gopal to keep notes?
3. Why did Melina use the word *lottery* about the place you are born in?
4. Explain the disagreement between Sukhvinder and Melina about living in Mongolia.
5. Is Sukhvinder justified in saying that poverty is relative?
6. Write an email to a local charity outlining your ideas for tackling poverty in your country.

Global Perspectives

To what extent is poverty an issue in your region or country? How does this compare to poverty on a more global scale? What systems would you recommend be put in place to discuss and start to resolve the issue of poverty on a local or regional level? In order to make poor people better off, does that mean making wealthier people less well off?

Understanding how a group works

Miss Favoro said I was the chair. I keep the discussion in order and, when people have had their say, I move the discussion on. Everyone must have a chance to say something. I sometimes make a summary of what has been said.

I had to keep notes and make a record of the discussion so we could report back. My job was to listen, and I needed to be a quick writer – which I wasn't.

They need Angelo and me to make intelligent ideas and explanations. I listen to the others and I agree or disagree with them.

I was very helpful when Melina didn't know 'dehydrate' and I finished her sentence for her. I think I had the best ideas.

You are Miss Favoro. You have heard the recording of the discussion. What would you say to each of the four students about the part they played in the discussion?

Speaking & Listening – group discussions

Discuss the following topics. Use what you have found out about the different parts people play in discussions and try to improve on the discussion you heard.

1. Discuss the importance of water to people all over the world, including:
   - why we need water
   - what happens when there is a drought and in places where there is a problem in getting enough water
   - how some disasters are caused by too much water.
2. Discuss what you understand by poverty and why it is a world problem. Make a short list of things you can discuss.

Remember

Listen carefully to other people when sharing ideas in a group discussion. If you take turns without interrupting, your group discussion will be much better!

Using a character to start a story

You've probably wondered how to start a story. One way is to present a character and let your story grow out of your description.

This is the beginning of a story called *The Ostler*. In the old days an ostler was the person who looked after travellers' horses when they stayed overnight at an inn.

The sleeping man

I find an old man, fast asleep, in one of the stalls of the stable. It is midday, and rather a strange time for an ostler to devote to sleep. Something curious, too, about the man's face. A withered woebegone face. The eyebrows painfully contracted; the mouth fast set, and drawn down at the corners; the hollow cheeks sadly, and, as I cannot help fancying, prematurely wrinkled; the scanty, grizzled hair, telling weakly its own tale of some past sorrow or suffering. How fast he draws his breath, too, for a man asleep! He is talking in his sleep.

'Wake up!' I hear him say, in a quick whisper through his fast-clenched teeth. 'Wake up there! Murder!'

From *The Ostler* by Wilkie Collins

Talk about what is interesting about the ostler. Does the extract suggest more to you than just describing what he looked like? How do you think the story might go on (and even finish?)

Here are some more characters who might start off a story…

Using vocabulary to create characters

1. Write the beginning of a story by describing a character. You can use an idea from one of the pictures on page 156, choose a picture of your own or create a character from your own imagination.

Appearance – What does your character look like?

Clothes – What is the character wearing?

Characteristics – What can you tell about the character from their appearance?

Speech – Does the character say anything and in what tone of voice?

Place – Where does your story take place?

Decide who is telling the story – you or somebody else?

How will you finish your description to lead on to what happens in the story?

You could start your description like this:

> As I turned the corner of the deserted side street, I was suddenly confronted by a most disturbing sight.

Or

> My uncle was a jolly person who had a habit of playing practical jokes on me. One day he was sitting at the table without his usual broad smile. His fingers drummed nervously on the table top and I could see that something was the matter.

Or

> There was a knock at the door and when I opened it there was the strangest person I had ever seen.

2. Now you have started your story, stop to think what might happen next and write this down. Remember to make your story grow out of what you have already written and be sure that your character plays a really important part.

WB

Test the skills you have used in this unit on page 75 of the Workbook.

Establish

After you complete this section, you will be able to:

- ➔ read a fictional text to understand how characterisation is created and used successfully
- ➔ respond appropriately to questions that require short but specific answers
- ➔ use carefully chosen quotations from a text to show engagement and understanding.

Tip

Before you answer questions, make sure you have understood the whole extract by reading it through very carefully. This is not a skimming exercise. You will be returning to the text repeatedly to scan for specific details.

Read this extract from a fiction text.

Coming home

Landing at the airport had confused Maria. Of course there was no airport when she was a child. She had left the farm when her parents fled the country thirty years ago and had settled a thousand miles away in a place that would protect them. Only now could she pluck up enough courage to return. She wondered where she had found the resolution to do so because she was not an outgoing person, but she needed to take perhaps her only chance to re-discover her roots.

'This way', said a kind voice as she threaded her way through the airport which seemed like a monster to her, ready to swallow her up.

She did not recognise the town. It had become a city with tramways where she remembered carts pulled by lumbering oxen, and smart business people where she remembered sad men by the roadside.

Kind people pointed the way to her village when she spoke its name, and Maria set off through tall, smart buildings that once were cornfields. They seemed never-ending, but she knew the farm was near.

Suddenly she saw it. She recognised the weathered, wooden buildings immediately. They appeared the same as ever, ramshackle, but friendly and welcoming. They looked insignificant, hemmed in by the grey faces of the tower blocks of the new university. Maria shed a tear for happy childhood days and entered the farmhouse.

Glossary

hemmed in surrounded by

ramshackle old, in need of repair

resolution strength of mind

'Yes?' demanded an unfriendly voice. 'What can I do for you?' The woman's face was wrinkled, saddened by time, yet she had the toughness of a farmer's wife. The two women looked at each other for a time, searching for recognition. Then suddenly, the old lady exclaimed with astonishment, 'It can't be! After all these years!' and flung her arms round Maria, weeping with amazement. In that moment, Maria recognised her aunt, the brave patriot who had refused to leave her country but stayed to keep the farm alive.

Later, she told her how the university bought the surrounding land, how they offered her money, but how she refused. 'You see, my dear, it was the family tradition. So many generations – I couldn't give it up. It is so good. I never thought to see you again.'

Tip

Take note of the punctuation used in dialogue as this will give you a clue to how the characters are behaving and the emotions they are feeling.

Engage

Questions often ask you to find a quotation to support your answer or to give a word or phrase from the passage that matches a statement. Questions are often about characters and settings. You may have to find examples of devices like personification, alliteration, onomatopoeia and imagery.

Answer the following questions to practise these skills.

1. What sort of person is Maria's aunt? Write one word or phrase in your own words. Give a quotation from the passage to support your answer.
2. Explain in your own words two ways in which the town had changed since Maria was last there.
3. Why did Maria start to cry when she saw the farmhouse?
4. Give two phrases from the passage that show the difference between the university buildings and the farm buildings.
5. Give one example of a simile and one of a metaphor from the passage.

Evaluate

Here is a selection of sample answers to the questions on the previous page. For each question, think about which answers are best and why.

1. What sort of person is Maria's aunt? Write one word or phrase in your own words. Give a quotation from the passage to support your answer.
   - **A** Unfriendly; quotation – 'demanded an unfriendly voice'
   - **B** Unhappy; quotation – 'saddened by time'
   - **C** Stubborn; quotation – 'refused to leave her country'; 'offered her money, but she refused'
2. Explain in your own words two ways in which the town had changed since Maria was last there.
   - **A** Everything looked more modern.
   - **B** She did not recognise it.
   - **C** There were a lot of businessmen.
   - **D** It was much bigger.
3. Why did Maria start to cry when she saw the farmhouse?
   - **A** Maria shed a tear for happy childhood days.
   - **B** Seeing the farmhouse suddenly brought happy memories back to her.
   - **C** She wanted to be a child again.
4. Give two phrases from the passage that show the difference between the university buildings and the farm buildings.
   - **A** 'Maria set off through tall, smart buildings that once were cornfields.'
   - **B** 'The same as ever, ramshackle…'
   - **C** 'The grey faces of the tower blocks'
   - **D** 'They looked insignificant'
5. Give one example of a simile and one of a metaphor from the passage.
   - **A** 'Like a monster' is a simile.
   - **B** 'The same as ever' is a simile.
   - **C** 'Lumbering' is a metaphor.
   - **D** 'Threaded' is a metaphor.

Tip

When reading questions requiring short answers, be careful to look for the key words in each question. If a question asks for information about how a place has changed, only provide details of what has changed and not just general information about the place.

Tip

Be careful to read the question! It asked for the difference.

Enable

At the beginning of this Assessment workshop, one of your targets was to respond appropriately to questions that require short but specific answers.

Read this extract. Haoyou is a 12-year-old boy whose story is set in China in the 13th century. Haoyou's father has been killed, so Haoyou must provide an income for his mother and baby sister.

The Kite-maker

So Haoyou became a kite-maker. Haoyou the artisan. Haoyou the breadwinner. Great-Uncle Bo (...), grudgingly gave money enough to buy some lengths of reject silk, some soiled paper, sewing thread, size, and a craft knife. Haoyou went out himself to cut bamboo, which he split into spills. He made red kites and blue ones, white kites and yellow.

'Where shall I put them?' he asked his mother, holding up the first, moving his hand back and forth so that the size-wet silk breathed like a diaphragm.

'In your father's bedroom,' said Qing'an. 'I'll sleep by the hearth.' Haoyou was shocked that his model-making should oust his mother from her bed, but obedience forbade him to argue. Besides, his heart thrilled at the thought his kites were adjudged so important. Up until now, they had simply been a hobby. Now they were his profession, and his mother walked among them as through a zoo of weird and wonderful animals.

As indeed, they were.

Haoyou made triangular kites and square ones, oblongs and pennons with swallow tails. He made box kites and tubular kites, and with every one, he mastered some new deftness, learned some secret trick of quickness, and how to keep waste to the minimum.

His friends said, 'Let's see what you made, Haoyou! Let's see.' But Haoyou only smiled that polite, businessman's smile which he had seen Great-Uncle Bo use: the yes which meant no. 'When I have enough,' he told them.

His mother – quiet-spoken at the best of times – trod the house as hesitantly as a crane, and said nothing. But he heard her murmur to the family shrine, where Pei's rice bowl stood, 'Do you see, Pei? Do you see how hard our boy is working?' And then the pride and honour pricked behind Haoyou's eyes and he vowed to make the most beautiful kites Dagu had ever seen.

From *The Kite Rider* by Geraldine McCaughrean

Tip

You may not understand every word in the text but you should be able to work out the approximate meaning of a word you do not know. Understanding the context – the sentence the word is in and other sentences around it – can be very useful.

Glossary

artisan skilled worker

spills thin strips

Follow up – answering questions on fiction

Answer these questions about using quotations accurately.

1. Which of these sentences shows the reader that Haoyou is the main source of income for his family? Tick (✓) **one** box.

'So Haoyou became a kite-maker.' ☐

'Haoyou the artisan.' ☐

'Haoyou the breadwinner.' ☐

2. What does the writer's use of the word *grudgingly* on line 2 suggest about Great-Uncle Bo's personality? Circle **one** answer from the list.

A He is generous and thoughtful.

B He is selfish and angry.

C He is mean and reluctant to help.

3. Look at lines 10–15.

a In your own words, explain how the writer emphasises the significance of Haoyou's kite-making through the actions of his mother and his own change of perspective.

- His mother: ……………………………………………………
- Haoyou: ……………………………………………………

b Give one quotation from lines 10–15 in support of each of your points.

- His mother: ……………………………………………………
- Haoyou: ……………………………………………………

4. On lines 15–16, what **two** kinds of literary device does the writer use in the phrase 'as through a zoo of weird and wonderful animals'? Tick (✓) **two** boxes.

Metaphor ☐

Simile ☐

Assonance ☐

Alliteration ☐

Hyperbole ☐

5. Look at lines 26–31. In your own words, explain what is physically happening to him when 'the pride and honour pricked behind Haoyou's eyes'.

Tip

Read the question very carefully. A question asking for a quotation requires you to find a specific word or phrase in the extract. It is testing your understanding in a different way to a question that asks you to answer in your own words.

6. How does the writer create a sense of growing excitement in the extract? Copy and complete the table by referring to the passage. You will need an explanation written in your own words and a relevant quotation.

	Quotation	Explanation
Using lists	'He made red kites and blue ones, white kites and yellow.'	
Using the rule of three		The writer increases the pace by grouping together actions to show an improvement in Haoyou's mastery of kite-making skills.

7. What does the writer infer by using the phrase 'businessman's smile' on line 23? Tick (✓) **one** box.

   Haoyou is being dishonest and evasive with his friends ☐

   Haoyou is unsure and frightened of how to behave ☐

   Haoyou is growing into his new role as a breadwinner ☐

8. Look at line 27. The phrase 'as hesitantly as a crane' is an example of what literary technique? Circle **one** answer from the list.

   A Metaphor

   B Simile

   C Synonym

9. What aspect of a crane is being used to describe the mother's actions?

10. In your own words, explain why it is most important that Haoyou can create such wonderful kites.

When you have finished, discuss your part of the story with your teacher.

Tip

When choosing quotations from an extract to answer a question, ask yourself the following questions:

- Does this quotation exactly match what the question is asking?
- Are there any alternative quotations to consider before choosing?
- How much of the chosen text is actually needed to answer the question fully?

9 The world today

In this unit, you will engage with some important issues in the world we live in today. You will read about the debate surrounding publication of gender-specific books and the effect they have on children's understanding of the world. You will also consider the potential threats to our planet caused by asteroids and global warming. You will listen to a stirring speech by a head teacher attempting to inspire her students. Finally, you will engage with two texts that explore the effect of advancing technology on our everyday lives.

And in doing all that, you will be practising these key skills:

Speaking & Listening

- Work within a group to discuss the issues you think are most important in the world today.
- Articulate and share ideas with a partner in order to complete question-setting tasks.

Writing

- Enhance writing by creating vivid images through the effective use of selected verbs.
- Use homonyms effectively when considering meaning in context.

Reading

- Understand the way implicit meaning is conveyed through inferred ideas in a text.
- Evaluate how writers use connotation and the effect it has in shaping meaning in a text.

Assessment workshop

You will gain practice in the key assessment skill of recognising different types of short-answer exam questions and understanding the specific skill each type of question is testing. You will also respond effectively to questions on non-fiction texts requiring short answers.

Thinking time

1. Note down some of the associations you think of when considering the world today. The pictures and the quotations in the speech bubbles may help you. Compare your ideas with a partner. How similar or different are they?
2. Does the world today please you? Write a list of what pleases you about the world today and another list of what makes you displeased. Discuss your lists with a partner. Together, think about the words that best describe your feelings of pleasure and displeasure.
3. Look at the quotation from Martin Luther King Junior. Although it is over half a century old, it seems even more relevant to the world today. With your partner, first discuss what you think he meant by his comment. Then think about these questions:
   - Has the age of the Internet now made our world even more geographically linked than Martin Luther King could ever have imagined?
   - Is the ease of communication afforded by the Internet a positive force for good or does it have a negative effect?

This unit will explore different aspects of the world today and also give you an opportunity to focus on some important skills moving forwards towards your exams.

"But I've learned that no one is too small to make a difference."
Greta Thunberg

"The world today doesn't please me."
Brigitte Bardot

"The world in which we live is geographically one. The challenge that we face today is to make it one in terms of brotherhood."
Martin Luther King Junior

Speaking & Listening – presenting your ideas

The climate activist Greta Thunberg is quoted as saying that "no one is too small to make a difference". Do you agree with this philosophy?

Prepare a short presentation that addresses what you can do in a small way to make a difference to the world today. You need to persuade an audience so be passionate and convincing in your argument.

When you have prepared your talk, share it with your partner or in a small group. Take note of the constructive feedback you receive.

Let books be books

The following editorial was published in the *Independent on Sunday* newspaper to explain its decision to no longer review books aimed specifically at just boys or just girls.

Gender-specific books demean all our children

A good read is just that. Ask any child, regardless of gender, says Independent on Sunday literary editor Katy Guest.

Sugar and spice and all things nice, that's what little girls are made of. And boys? They're made of trucks and trains and aeroplanes, building blocks, chemistry experiments, sword fights and guns, football, cricket, running and jumping, adventure and ideas, games … and pretty much anything else they can think of.

At least, that's the impression that children are increasingly given by the very books that are supposed to broaden their horizons.

An online campaign called Let Books Be Books, which petitions publishers to **ditch** gender-specific children's books, has met with mixed success recently. Last week, both Paragon (which sells Disney titles, among others) and Usborne (the Independent Publisher of the Year 2014) agreed that they will no longer publish books specifically titled 'for boys' or 'for girls'. Unfortunately, Michael O'Mara, which owns Buster Books, pledged to continue segregating younger readers according to their gender. Mr O'Mara himself told *The Independent* that their *Boys' Book* covers "things like how to make a bow and arrow and how to play certain sports and you'd get things about style and how to look **cool** in the girls' book." At the same time, he added: "We would never publish a book that demeaned one sex or the other".

It is not like a publisher to leave a **bandwagon unjumped** upon, but Mr O'Mara seems to have missed a trick. Hasn't he heard of Suzanne Collins' **multi-million-selling** *Hunger Games* trilogy, which has a female lead character and striking, non-pink cover designs, and is loved by boys and girls equally? For anyone else who has missed it, the heroine, Katniss Everdeen, is rather **handy** with a bow and arrow and doesn't spend much time caring about looking cool. At the same time, Mr O'Mara should know that telling boys they should all be interested in doing physical activities outdoors, while girls should be interested in how they look, is demeaning to both.

There are those who will say that insisting on gender-neutral books and toys for children is a bizarre experiment in social engineering by radical **lefties** and paranoid "**femininazies**" who won't allow boys to be boys, and girls to be girls. (Because, by the way, seeking equality of rights and opportunities was a key plank of Nazi ideology, was it?) But the experiment is nothing new. When I grew up in the 1970s, and when my parents grew up in the 1950s, brothers and sisters shared the same toys, books and games, which came in many more colours than just pink and blue, and there was no obvious disintegration of society as a result.

Understanding

1. According to the article, what are little girls made of?
2. What does the term *gender-specific* mean?
3. Why might Mr O'Mara have 'missed a trick' in not supporting the new initiative?
4. What main point is the writer trying to make in the last paragraph?
5. How successful do you think the editorial is in justifying the decision taken by the writer? Explain your answer.
6. Write an email to Katy Guest in response to the editorial either agreeing with her viewpoint or arguing against it.

Word builder

1. *Multi*, as used in 'multi-million-selling', is an abbreviation of *multiple* meaning many. Think of five other words beginning with *multi*.
2. *Femininazies* is a portmanteau word from *feminine* and *Nazi*, used as an unflattering term to describe those who strongly believe in feminism. Try to explain why it is so unflattering.
3. *Bandwagon* is an informal word that has more than one meaning. In this editorial it means trend or fashion. What do you think is the original literal meaning of the word?
4. *Ditch* is also used informally but has another more formal literal meaning. The noun *ditch* describes a trench or waterway. What does it mean as a verb in the editorial?

Developing your language – counter-argument and the use of humour

In this editorial, Katy Guest injects humour through informal language, mostly used to describe the counter-argument to her own point of view. This makes her own argument seem more serious and therefore more important.

Match each informal word to its implied meaning:

a unjumped	fashionable – but used to mock the speaker
b lefties	skilled – used as an understatement
c cool	socialists – used as part of an exaggerated explanation
d handy	ignored – a made-up word showing sarcasm for the subject

Word cloud

bandwagon
cool
ditch
femininazies
handy
lefties
multi-million-selling
unjumped

Glossary

broaden their horizons increase their expectations

gender-neutral not specific to male or female

petitions (verb) formally requests

social engineering organised social change in a society

Remember

Often a piece of writing will contain both literal meaning – what is actually said – and implied meaning – an idea that is hinted at but must be interpreted by the reader.

Making deductions and recognising meaning

When responding to a text you have to understand not only what is stated explicitly but any implied meaning that lies beneath the actual words. You have to infer what you think the writer means. This is a skill that often takes some thought.

What is the difference between implicit meaning and inference?

Implicit meaning

This is what the writer implies.

The meaning is not made clear through just the words alone. In non-fiction texts, context and tone often give clues as to this indirect meaning.

Inference

This is what the reader infers.

The reader works out what the intended meaning is from the clues given by the writer. The reader has to make judgments based on these clues.

Inferring implied meaning

Look again at lines 4–9 in Katy Guest's editorial.

The explicit meaning suggests that the genetic make-up of girls consists of pleasant cookery ingredients but boys are made of all kinds of different and exciting things. Of course, neither statement is accurate so the explicit meaning does not help you to understand what the writer really means. To do this you need to infer the implied meaning.

1. To infer the implied meaning, match each statement to the correct clue given by the writer:

a The part use of a nursery rhyme	suggests opportunities for boys are endless
b The short list for girls	suggests boys traditionally have more choices
c The extended list for boys	creates a whimsical tone
d The use of an ellipsis (…)	implies girls are limited by traditional perceptions

2. 'And pretty much anything else <u>they</u> can think of.'

Why is the pronoun *they* used instead of *we*? Who is *they* referring to?

3. Having put the clues together, what have you inferred about the writer's opinion on the way girls and boys have been traditionally viewed?
4. Now look at lines 11–13. Try answering the following questions to infer the meaning and build up your understanding.
   - **a** Why is this sentence on its own as a separate paragraph?
   - **b** What is the significance of using *increasingly*?
   - **c** What is the inclusion of *very* used to emphasise?
   - **d** Why is the use of *supposed* important?

Providing evidence to support inference

To support your ideas about inferred meaning in a text, you should provide some evidence either as a statement in your own words or as a direct quotation from the text.

Further into the editorial (lines 33–47), Katy Guest responds to the opinions of a publisher she clearly disagrees with.

1. Find quotations from lines 33–47 to support the following:
   - **a** Publishers choose to publish books that follow trends rather than anything original.
   - **b** Rhetorical questioning
   - **c** Use of made up word to add comedic effect
   - **d** Informal use of language to lighten the tone
   - **e** Using Mr O'Mara's own words from a previous paragraph to criticise his opinions
   - **f** Repeated overly polite reference to the subject of her disapproval
   - **g** Criticism of traditional colours attributed to gender.

Implied meaning in fiction

Fiction writers also build implied meaning through indirect statements about characters and situations in much the same way.

Discuss what you can infer from the extract on the right, and why, about:

- **a** how the boy feels
- **b** what the head teacher is like
- **c** why the boy is meeting the head teacher.

Global Perspectives

Are there situations in your local and regional area where you feel opportunities are being denied because of gender? Research whether these situations are particular to a cultural understanding in your regional area or more part of a global issue. What changes would you suggest in order to make gender opportunity more equal?

Remember

Writers imply meaning and readers infer meaning.

The boy shivered slightly as he reluctantly entered the head teacher's office. His eyes darted from side to side with increasing frequency as he inched closer to the tyrant's desk. Guilty flashes of regret punctuated his more immediate thoughts on what lay ahead.

Asteroids: between a rock and a hard place

Are asteroids a real danger to the Earth? This extract from a newspaper article seems to think so.

In February 2013, a large asteroid **ripped** over the Chelyabinsk district of Russia, trailing cartoonish lines of smoke as it made its shallow entry, **radiating** so much light and heat that onlookers were left with reddened faces. Skin peel. When the asteroid **exploded**, 15 miles up, there was a terrible, prolonged bang – a noise that has rung on, in its own way, ever since.

We now know that the explosion over Chelyabinsk occurred with a force equal to 500 kilotons of TNT, or a couple of dozen Nagasaki bombs. Had it come down a little steeper that February, directing the might of its detonation at rather than over Chelyabinsk, the asteroid would have killed thousands on the ground. A little later, it might have done for many more in Moscow, or Riga, or Gothenburg. Though nobody died at Chelyabinsk, it was an event of such calamitous potential that the asteroid was classified by certain astronomers as a 'city-killer'. Those astronomers have wondered since, if we're not being a little complacent.

In November last year, having had months to chew on the data from Chelyabinsk, a Nasa scientist called Bill Cooke said the likely frequency of such meteor strikes was being re-evaluated. That month, a trio of studies published in the journals *Nature* and *Science* suggested impacts of Chelyabinsk's magnitude were between three and 10 times more likely to happen than previously supposed. The UN, in December, called

Largest part of the Chelyabinsk meteorite

for the creation of an international asteroid warning network. Come the new year, it took only hours for the first major rock of 2014 to arrive: a car-sized lump that **burst** apart over the Atlantic on 1 January.

To recap: asteroids are hunks of space rock that whisk around the solar system in orbits around the sun, **colliding** with anything that crosses their path. If they collide with Earth, we call them meteorites. Most are small and burn up in our atmosphere; some are big enough to matter, such as the Chelyabinsk rock, which was the size of a swimming pool, 20m from end to end. Though Nasa has for some time been tracking giant asteroids (those at least 1km wide), it has never seemed much concerned about lesser rocks – those capable only of **scraping** away a city, say.

At a press conference earlier this year, former Nasa astronaut Dr Edward Lu announced that there are around 1m asteroids in the Earth's vicinity "with the potential to destroy a major metropolitan area". He teed up an animated graphic to demonstrate how unprepared we are. The graphic showed the Earth in orbit among the dangerous asteroids we knew about and were tracking, around 10,000 of them. Seen like this, our planet looked like a pedestrian **hustling** along a busy street, not overly troubled. Then Lu changed the graphic to show "what it really looks like out there" – the Earth **ploughing** on through a million-strong field of city-killing asteroids. I saw the same pedestrian, now trying to make it across a train station concourse in the middle of rush hour, avoiding collisions purely by fluke. "Blind luck," as Lu put it.

This information, I thought, watching online, was appalling. Why wasn't it all over the nightly news? I can't be the only person who feels fidgety on the subject, having watched *Deep Impact* and *Armageddon* at an impressionable age. I watched some of the YouTube videos of the Chelyabinsk strike, dozens of them recorded on mobile phones, and found that though the images were shocking (people swept flat by the shock of the impact), it was the noise that was truly unbearable.

Understanding

1. In what country is the district of Chelyabinsk located?
2. What is the difference between an asteroid and a meteorite?
3. Why didn't Nasa consider it important to track the Chelyabinsk meteorite in space?
4. What impact do the quotations from Nasa scientists have on how the reader responds to the article?
5. Instead of opening with an explanation, the writer does not discuss the nature of asteroids until paragraph 4. Is this an effective way of shaping the article?
6. Does this article convince you that asteroids provide a greater threat to life on Earth than climate change? Write an email to the writer, outlining your views on this.

Word cloud

burst **ploughing**
colliding **radiating**
exploded **ripped**
hustling **scraping**

Word builder

1. The writer uses the verb *ploughing*, often used in a farming context, to describe how Earth moves through the asteroid field. Why is this an appropriate connection to make?
2. How does the writer's use of the verb *radiating* effectively link the comparison between the Chelyabinsk asteroid and the bomb dropped on the city of Nagasaki in 1945?
3. The writer uses a simile likening Earth's movement through space to 'a pedestrian hustling along a busy street'. Why is the use of *hustling* as a verb more effective than using *moving*?

Glossary

Armageddon a disaster movie

Deep Impact a disaster movie

Nagasaki Japanese city on which an atomic bomb was dropped in 1945

Nasa North American Space Agency (NASA)

TNT an explosive

Developing your language – using connotations to create images

The term *city-killer*, used to describe an asteroid, has connotations of mass destruction and associated suffering. Cities have large populations so destroying one would be a major disaster.

Look at how the verbs *burst*, *exploded* and *ripped* are used in the text:

- 'a car-sized lump that burst apart …'
- 'When the asteroid exploded …'
- 'a large asteroid ripped over …'

Each time, the choice of verb creates a violent image to help the reader visualise the destructive power of the asteroid.

1. Copy and complete the table to match a connotation to each verb.

Verb	Suggested connotation
burst	
exploded	
ripped	

2. Look at the way the verb *colliding* is used in the article to describe the movement of asteroids in space:

> '… asteroids are hunks of space rock that whisk around the solar system in orbits around the sun, colliding with anything that crosses their path.'

a What is the definition of *colliding*?

b What connotations are suggested by using the verb in this article?

c How might using the verbs in the box instead of *colliding* change the connotations suggested?

3. Describing a meteorite as potentially 'scraping away a city' seems to be an odd phrase to use.

a What image do you visualise when reading the phrase 'scraping away a city'?

b Comment on the use of the word *scraping* in describing the movement of the meteorite as it contacts the city.

Global Perspectives

Unlike war or poverty, climate change and the threat of asteroids are hard to quantify unless you are directly affected. How seriously are these issues taken in your local region or at national level? Research the threat that either issue presents and compare the impact locally to that globally. What can individuals do to bring about positive change?

brushing *evading*
threatening *nudging*

c Which of these phrases would you more readily associate with the verb *scraping*?

- Scraping rain from an umbrella
- Scraping ice from a frozen car window
- Scraping water from a bottle

d Why don't the connotations suggested by the phrases you rejected in question 3c work successfully?

e Suggest three other phrases where using *scraping* may be appropriate.

Connotations in context

Connotations often depend on the context. For example, reaction to a disaster movie can suggest different connotations depending on who the viewer is.

Positive connotations

Excitement – enthralled by the developing storyline

Enjoyment – engaged by the concept

Thrills – loving the fast-paced action sequences and epic scenarios

Anticipation – unable to wait to find out what happens in the end

Negative connotations

Apprehension – nervous about the concept

Fear – for the characters or the developing scenario

Incredulity – thinking the concept is ridiculous and too far-fetched

Depression – wondering if the destruction could really happen

Now it is your turn. What differing connotations can be suggested by the following ideas?

a A solitary astronaut in space looking back at Earth

b A space explorer encountering alien life for the first time

c A small child watching a comet pass over her home

Use a spider diagram, as started below, to note connotations for each idea. This is a useful way of planning because you can decide on the order after the diagram is completed.

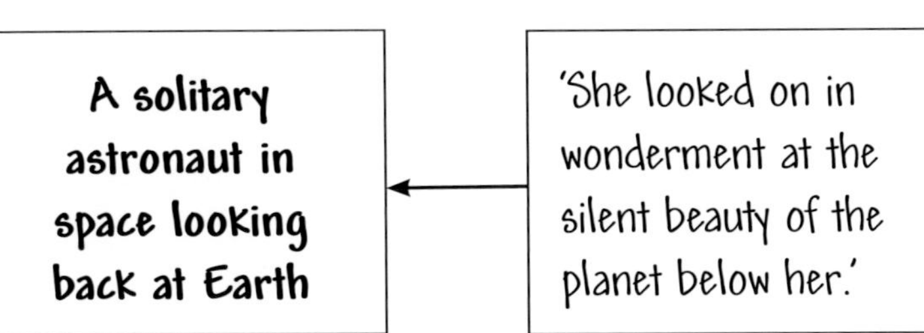

A solitary astronaut in space looking back at Earth
'She looked on in wonderment at the silent beauty of the planet below her.'

New beginnings

Listen to the speech by a head teacher addressing students in her school at the beginning of a new school year. The address is intended to motivate the students and inspire them to succeed in their studies.

Once you have listened to the speech for the first time, make a note of the three main ideas it is based on. Think of these as sub-headings within the speech much as you would topic sentences in a written piece. These notes will provide you with an overall understanding of what the speech is about and how it has been structured.

Take your notes on the three main ideas and add another sub-heading – 'The marshmallow challenge'.

Listen to the recording again with your notes in front of you. This time, add two bullet points to each of the sub-headings to represent the key points within each one. It can be difficult to distinguish the main ideas from the supporting detail but this method is one way of doing so.

Listen to the audio for this task:

Remember

This method works equally well when responding to a written text. Always read the text more than once to understand its content better.

Understanding

1. What does the head teacher say the first day back at school is like?
2. Why does the head teacher use the metaphor 'reaching for the stars' to inspire her students?
3. Explain in your own words what the 'marshmallow challenge' is.
4. What is the purpose of using quotations from famous people to promote the first two main ideas in the speech?
5. Of the three main ideas the head teacher explains in her speech, which one do you think is the most important key to achieving success in your studies? Explain your answer.
6. Write a list of five to ten bullet points for success based on your own experience and aspirations.

Glossary

aspirations future hopes/goals

marshmallow a light, very soft and chewy sweet

'ta da' informal expression of achievement

'uh oh' informal expression of failure

Word builder

Look at the six words in the Word cloud. Each word has more than one meaning so they are examples of homonyms. Often the intended meaning is made clear by the context and whether the word is being used as a noun, adjective or verb.

1. Here are the meanings of the words as used in the speech. Use a dictionary, if needed, to find an alternative meaning for each one.
   - **a** a well-known team challenge (noun) – a competition
   - **b** to be in charge (noun) – to be in command
   - **c** Until you crack it (informal verb) – until you succeed
   - **d** to work in a team is critical (adjective) – of crucial importance
   - **e** letting someone else execute it (verb) – put into effect
   - **f** Not as easy as it sounds (verb) – seems
2. **a** You may have found that there are multiple meanings for each word, depending on the context. Take *charge*, for example. Which of the following are correct definitions of the word?
   - A fee for an item or service
   - To rush at the enemy in battle
   - To fill with electrical current
   - To be in control
   - To load ammunition into a firearm

   b Write three sentences in which you use the word *sounds* in different contexts to those you've already encountered in this section.

Word cloud

challenge	critical
charge	execute
crack	sounds

Remember

Context is key to understanding. Without it, words can have different meanings and this may result in misunderstanding.

Developing your language – using homonyms

Here are some more examples of homonyms. Look at these words and discuss the different meanings they can have.

bank	examine	quarry	cast
express	refuse	cataract	palm
rock	entrance	pupil	scrap

WB

Test the skills you have used in this unit on page 88 of the Workbook.

Establish

After you complete this section, you will be able to:

- ➔ recognise some of the literary and language features used in non-fiction writing
- ➔ make relevant choices when selecting information to respond to specific situations
- ➔ develop your understanding of how short-answer questions (other than multiple-choice questions) are constructed, by considering key aspects of the various different types.

Start by reading this personal account by a writer discovering the joys of owning an iPod and trying to decide what music to upload.

iPod, therefore I am: a personal journey through music

The process of deciding what to upload was tantamount to listening to every song I'd ever bought.

Some were imported immediately but many more were forced to walk my PowerBook's metaphorical plank. Would I rip it into an MP3 or press eject?

Over the next six months, I began loading my iPod as though my life depended on it. Not only did I go through every single CD and upload the songs I liked, I also recorded all of my vinyl and then began downloading songs from the Internet (legally, of course).

In the space of just a few months I was totally addicted.

I fell in love with the process immediately. As soon as the song was uploaded, the file just lay there, nameless, blameless.

And so I would type in the artist's name, the song title, the album it came from (as well as a host of other categories) and then watch it flip into its rightful alphabetical place.

And having spent a few nights doing this, my friend Robin, who had already become well versed in the ways of the iPod, said I should upload while connected to the Internet, as the program would then download the information for you.

Fantastic! My own private radio station was being compiled right before my eyes – all I had to do was upload the content.

As soon as I got busy with my new toy, experts popped up everywhere … Was I going to start burning CDs, 70 minutes of personalised taste to give to friends and family? Was I going to move up a gear and burn my first MP3 CD, a full eight-and-a-half hours of compressed digital fun? How was I doing with smart playlists? Was I making my own CD covers yet?

This was all before me, as what I was really enjoying was editing my life.

This is an autobiographical account written in the first person. It is meant to be both informative and entertaining.

When responding to a non-fiction text, you need to pay close attention to both explicit and implicit meaning. This may include the writer's use of imagery as well as the way language and structure have been used for effect to construct the viewpoint.

Tip

Test and exam questions always include a portion of time allowed purely for reading. Make good use of this time both at the start and when checking your answers at the end.

Engage

Below are the types of short-answer questions based on a non-fiction text or extract which you will see in a typical exam. In most short-answer questions you will also be given a paragraph and/or line reference to direct you to the relevant section of the text. It is really important you pay attention to these references as they are included to help you.

Tip

In multiple-choice questions, you will be given choices for your answer.

In other short-answer questions, you will not be given choices.

Study the questions and possible answers below and on the next page. Think about what type of questions they are and what kind of response each one is looking for.

1. Give one example of technical language associated with computers used in the first paragraph.

Possible answers: process; upload; tantamount

2. In the second paragraph, what does the verb *rip* mean?

Possible answers: to tear apart; to transfer to a digital format; to break

3. Give an example of a simile used in the third paragraph.

Possible answers: 'as though my life depended on it'; 'Not only did I go through every single CD'; 'As soon as the song was uploaded'

4. Give one example of a conjugated irregular verb on line 9.

Possible answers: love; fell; lay

5. What idea links lines 9–15?

Possible answers: choosing albums to transform into MP3 tracks; the writer's enjoyment of preparing his iPod catalogue; all the mistakes the writer made when uploading

6. Give two structural features of an autobiographical text that can be found in this text?

Possible answers: it is written in the first person; it is written in a formal style; ideas are organised into paragraphs; it is written in third person; it uses sub-headings

7. What is the viewpoint in this text?

Possible answers: first person; second person; third person

Tip

Line numbers will be printed in the margin of the text but you may also need to know which paragraph is being referenced in a question. After reading the text for the first time, number the paragraphs in the other margin. This will save you time when answering the questions.

Evaluate

How did you manage with the seven questions in the Engage section? Did you find it quite straightforward to locate the correct parts of the text to answer each question? Were you clear as to what each question was asking you to do?

Here are the answers to the questions, together with some comments on each type of question and what it was testing.

In groups, discuss and agree on three more possible answers: a strong (correct) answer; an answer that is a good attempt but not correct; and an answer that is clearly wrong. To make it easier, your answers need not come from the extract.

1. The answer is *upload*.

   This is a vocabulary question. You were asked to find a technical word specifically associated with computers. Whilst *processor* may have been an option, if it had been included in the text, *process* is a more general term that has many contexts. *Tantamount* is an adjective meaning equal to or the same as, so is not a technical term.

2. The answer is 'to transfer to a digital format'.

   This is another vocabulary question but testing your understanding of context as well. *Rip* can also mean *to tear apart* and, more loosely, *to break* but neither definition fits the way *rip* is used in the context of the paragraph. Here it is used in the context of digital editing.

3. The answer is 'as though my life depended on it'.

   This is a literary techniques question. You need to know the difference between literary techniques so you can recognise them easily. A simile uses *as* or *like* to compare one idea to another. 'Not only did I go through every single CD' is a statement that does not compare two ideas though it is from the stated paragraph.

   There are two reasons why 'As soon as the song was uploaded' is not the correct answer. It is in paragraph 5, not paragraph 3, and it is not a comparison even though it begins with *as*.

4. The answer is *fell*.

   This is a grammar question that tests your knowledge of verbs and how they work. A conjugated verb is any that has been altered from its root form – in this case to signify tense. An irregular verb is one that does not follow normal rules when changing its form; for example, the past tense of *fall* is *fell* (not *falled*). *Lay* is also an irregular verb but is not on line 9. *Love* is used in this context as an abstract noun and not a verb.

5. The answer is: the writer's enjoyment of preparing his iPod's catalogue.

   This is an understanding question that tests whether you can recognise a central idea. In the first sentence on line 12, the writer writes about falling in love with the process. *Enjoyment* is associated with *love* and *preparation* is a *process*. The use of *And* to begin the next two paragraphs suggests the ideas are linked to the previous paragraph as a list might be.

6. The answers are: written in the first person; ideas organised into paragraphs.

   This is a question about structure. The text is autobiographical so must be written in the first person. If it were written in the third person, it would be a biography instead. A quick glance at the text will tell you that it is organised into paragraphs, short as they may be. It is mostly written in a formal style but there are phrases which are less formal, such as 'totally addicted', 'nameless, blameless' and 'Fantastic!' An autobiography may include sub-headings but there are none present in this extract.

7. The answer is: first person.

   This is a question about structure but also about viewpoint.

Tip

Unless you are absolutely certain, always consider alternatives when answering questions in a test. Even when you are certain of the answer, go back to the question to make sure your answer fulfils what the question is specifically asking you to do with the text.

Enable

At the beginning of this Assessment workshop, one of your targets was to recognise the different types of short-answer questions based on a non-fiction text or extract that you will respond to in an exam and to understand the specific skills each question is testing. You will now develop your understanding further by constructing your own range of questions.

Read this information text. In this blog post, the writer explores the possibilities made available through recent advances in 3D printing technology. Can we really print food?

Is 3D food printing the next microwave?

I've spent the last few years attempting to make logical sense of 3D printing, let alone printing of food! My brain just could not come to terms with it so the never-ending spiral of pondering just continued. But, no matter how many times I fail to come to a conclusion about this topic, the reverie keeps coming back up so I figured it was time to finally get down to the bottom of it and actually do some research. In my investigation for this post however, I started to question myself… did my lack of ability to understand the concept cause me to get behind the technology of the times? The majority of news coverage and articles started back in 2015, even citing studies and prototypes prior to that! This is not a new trend necessarily, but one that actually has a lot of momentum surrounding it and might even be here to stay. So back to business… what exactly is food printing?

Here is how it works

So, in the conventional way that we come to understand printing, your printer (or machine) is impressing ink (a liquid) onto a piece of paper (a surface). When we print off a sheet of paper the printer only needs to make that impression once and voila! You have a beautifully printed sheet of paper! So, what if your printer made that impression with the ink over and over again on the same spot? You would assume that the ink locations will get bulkier and you will start to see it rise from the paper… do you see where I am going with this? Suddenly with each layer you begin to find yourself creating something in three dimensions! Boom! We have 3D printing!

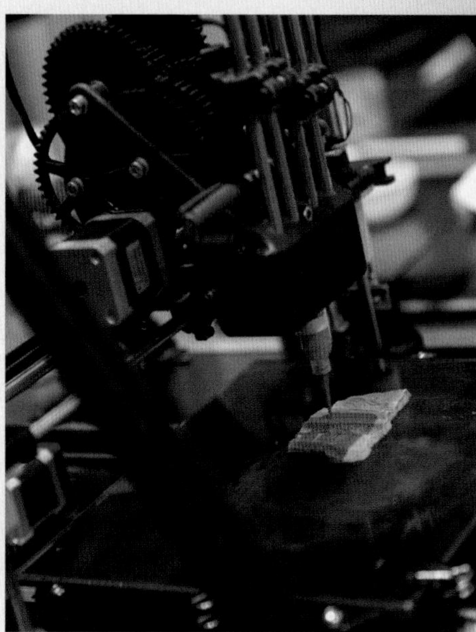

Now, I recognize that I am personally obsessed with anything that manipulates food or our perception of the world we live in and, others, maybe not so much. So, if you belong in the latter group, you are probably wondering what the point is to printing food. Why not just make it like we normally do? What is the advantage to this trend? What does it afford us? Granted, even though 3D printing might be a strange concept to grasp, once you do you will realize that with this method… the applications are endless. You're in complete control – so let your imagination run wild! One author claimed that 3D food printing could revolutionize the industry due to its ability to manipulate shape, colour, flavour, texture and nutrition (Sun et al. 2015). The capabilities are truly astounding. If you think of it like your normal printer, you can tell the printer exactly what you want it to print and boom – it does it! This 3D printing works the same way. You tell it what design you want to make and boom – there you go! You want something that resembles an apple yet tastes like cherry – you can do that! You want to make a pizza – why not! How about an intrinsically detailed decoration for your wedding cake – you bet!

Kenzi Hannum

Follow up – understanding short-answer questions

Respond to the following task.

Working on your own, create questions related to the text on 3D food printing. For each question, the skill has been identified below. You need to think carefully about how to phrase each question and produce a correct answer for each one.

Vocabulary questions

First refresh your knowledge of how vocabulary questions were worded in the Engage section. You may find a dictionary is a useful reference tool for this.

1. Write a vocabulary question to test understanding of the adjective *spiral* in paragraph 1.
2. Write a vocabulary question to test understanding of the noun *prototypes* in paragraph 1.
3. Write a vocabulary question to test understanding of another word elsewhere in the text. You could test understanding of 'voila', 'manipulates', 'revolutionise' or 'intrinsically', or any other word.

Literary techniques questions

First refresh your knowledge of how literary techniques questions were worded in the Engage section.

1. Write a question which tests literary techniques and identifies the repeated use of an onomatopoeic word in paragraphs 2 and 3.
2. Write a question which tests literary techniques and identifies the use of a triplet of questions in paragraph 3. (Look at lines 20–22.)

Tip

Whether you are constructing questions or trying to find the answers to those you have been given, always check that the answer fits the question exactly and that there are no alternatives you should also consider.

3. Write a question which tests literary techniques from elsewhere in the text. You could look for examples of the use of hyperbole or triplets, for example.

Grammar questions

First refresh your knowledge of how grammar questions were worded in the Engage section.

1. Write a grammar question that tests understanding of the use of ellipsis in paragraph 1.
2. Write a grammar question that tests understanding of why the writer uses parentheses (brackets) in paragraph 2.
3. Write a question that focuses on grammar from elsewhere in the text.

Understanding questions

First refresh your knowledge of how understanding questions were worded in the Engage section.

1. Write a question which tests understanding of the text and identifies the writer's excitement in paragraph 2 on finally comprehending how 3D printing works.
2. Write a question which tests understanding of the text and identifies two reasons why the 3D printing of food has huge potential, as explained in paragraph 3.
3. Write a question which tests understanding of the text. You could focus on explicit and implicit meaning in the main heading; the writer's dilemma; the differences between conventional and 3D printing; or the reason the writer believes that 3D printing of food will change the food industry.

Structure questions

First refresh your knowledge of how structure questions were worded in the Engage section.

1. Write a question which tests the structural features of the text and identifies the use of paragraphs to organise the text logically.
2. Write a question which tests the structural features of the text and identifies the use of sub-headings to organise the text appropriately.

Tip

Questions that ask you to use your own words will always explain this in the exam. If the question does not explicitly state that you need to use your own words, then you can safely assume you can use quotations and words from the text.

3. Write a question which tests different structural features used in the text. You could focus on the use of direct questions, switching narrative voice, the use of lists, or the use of informal language for humour.

In your own words questions

Tip

'In your own words' does not mean every word in your answer must paraphrase the text. Some words in the text – usually nouns, such as the names of characters or locations – can be used if there are no accurate substitutes.

1. Write a question that tests understanding of the excitement felt by the writer in paragraph 2 and requires answering using your own words.
2. Write a question that tests understanding of the reasons given in paragraph 3 for why 3D printing might be considered just an unnecessary trend and requires answering in your own words.
3. Write a question that specifically asks for a response 'using your own words', based on another part of the text.

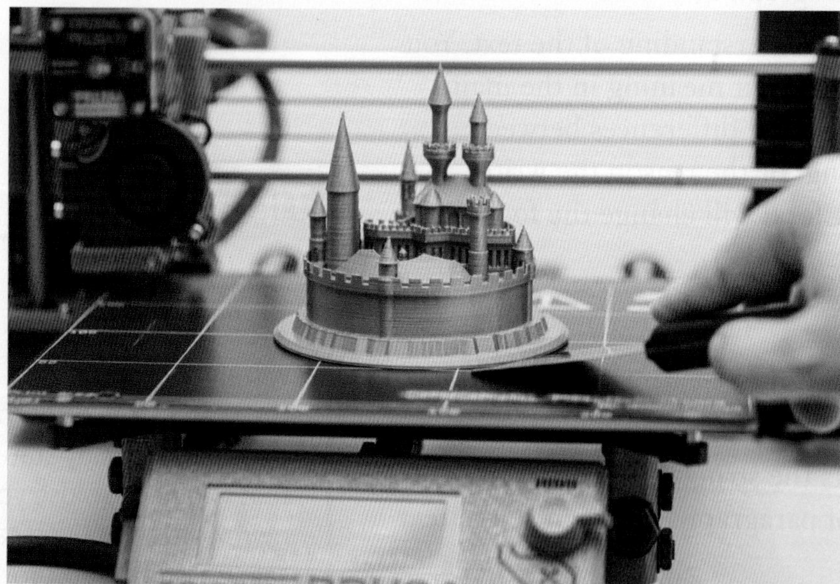

When you have finished, discuss your questions with your teacher.

Language and literacy reference

Active voice versus passive voice – Verbs are active when the subject of the sentence (the agent) does the action. Example: *The shark swallowed the fish*. Active verbs are used more in informal speech or writing.

Verbs are passive when the subject of the sentence has the action done to it. Example: *The fish was swallowed by the shark*. Passive verbs are used in more formal writing such as reports. Examples: *An eye-witness was interviewed by the police. Results have been analysed by the sales team.*

Sometimes turning an active sentence to passive, or vice versa, simply means moving the agent:

- The shark (agent and subject) + verb = active
- The fish (object) + verb = passive

Adjective – An adjective describes a noun or adds to its meaning. They are usually found in front of a noun. Example: *Green emeralds and glittering diamonds*. Adjectives can also come after a verb. Examples: *It was big*. *They looked hungry*. Sometimes you can use two adjectives together. Example: *tall and handsome*. This is called an adjectival phrase.

Adjectives can be used to describe degrees of intensity. To make a comparative adjective you usually add *–er* (or use *more*). Examples: *quicker*; *more beautiful*. To make a superlative you add *–est* (or use *most*). Examples: *quickest*; *most beautiful*.

Adverb – An adverb adds further meaning to a verb. Many are formed by adding *–ly* to an adjective. Example: *slow/slowly*. They often come next to the verb in a sentence. Adverbs can tell the reader: how – *quickly*, *stupidly*, *amazingly*; where – *there*, *here*, *everywhere*; when – *yesterday*, *today*, *now*; how often – *occasionally*, *often*.

Adverbial phrase – The part of a sentence that tells the reader when, where or how something happens is called an adverbial phrase. It is a group of words that functions as an adverb. Example: *I'm going to the dentist tomorrow morning* (when); *The teacher spoke to us as if he was in a bad mood* (how); *Sam ran all the way home* (where). These adverbials are called adverbials of time, manner and place.

Alliteration – Alliteration occurs when two or more nearby words start with the same sound. Example: *A slow, sad, sorrowful song*.

Antecedent – An antecedent is the person or thing to which the pronoun refers back. Example: *President Alkira realised that his life was in danger*. 'President Alkira' is the antecedent here.

Antonym – An antonym is a word or phrase that means the opposite of another word or phrase in the same language. Example: *shut* is an antonym of *open*. Synonyms and antonyms can be used to add variation and depth to your writing.

Audience – The readers of a text and/or the people for whom the author is writing; the term can also apply to those who watch a film or to television viewers.

Clause – A clause is a group of words that contains a subject and a verb. Example: *I ran*. In this clause, *I* is the subject and *ran* is the verb.

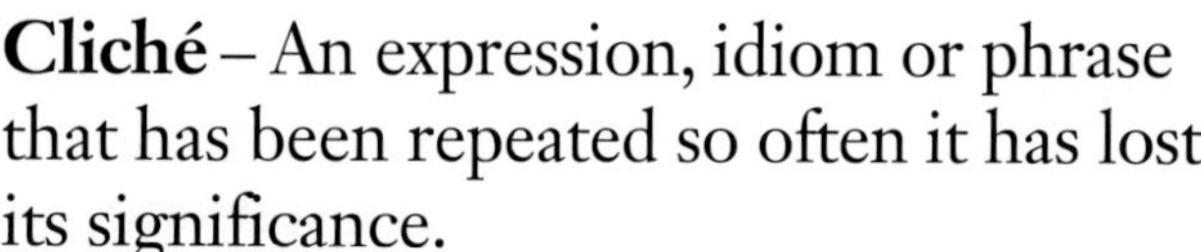

Cliché – An expression, idiom or phrase that has been repeated so often it has lost its significance.

Colloquial language – Informal, everyday speech as used in conversation; it may include slang expressions. Not appropriate in written reports, essays or exams.

Colon – A colon is a punctuation mark (:) used to indicate that an example, explanation or list is being used by the writer within the sentence. Examples: *You will need: a notebook, a pencil, a notepad and a ruler. I am quick at running: as fast as a cheetah.*

Conditional tense – This tense is used to talk about something that might happen. Conditionals are sometimes called 'if' clauses. They can be used to talk about imaginary situations or possible real-life scenarios. Examples: *If it gets any colder the river will freeze. If I had a million pounds I would buy a zoo.*

Conjugate – To change the tense or subject of a verb.

Conjunction – A conjunction is a word used to link clauses within a sentence such as: *and, but, so, until, when, as.* Example: *He had a book in his hand when he stood up.*

Connectives – A connective is a word or a phrase that links clauses or sentences. Connectives can be conjunctions. Example: *but, when, because.* Connectives can also be connecting adverbs. Example: *then, therefore, finally.*

Continuous tense – This tense is used to tell you that something is continuing to happen. Example: *I am watching football.*

Discourse markers – Words and phrases such as *on the other hand, to sum up, however,* and *therefore* are called discourse markers because they mark stages along an argument. Using them will make your paragraphs clearer and more orderly.

Exclamation – An exclamation shows someone's feelings about something. Example: *What a pity*!

Exclamation mark – An exclamation mark makes a phrase or a short sentence stand out. You usually use it in phrases like 'How silly I am!' and more freely in dialogue when people are speaking. Don't use it at the end of a long, factual sentence, and don't use it too often.

Idiom – An idiom is a colourful expression which has become fixed in the language. It is a phrase which has a meaning that cannot be worked out from the meanings of the words in it. Examples: '*in hot water*' means 'in trouble'; '*It's raining cats and dogs*' means 'it's raining heavily'.

Imagery – A picture in words, often using a metaphor or simile (figurative language) which describes something in detail: writers use visual, aural (auditory) or tactile imagery to convey how something looks, sounds or feels in all forms of writing, not just fiction or poetry. Imagery helps the reader to feel like they are actually there.

Irregular verb – An irregular verb does not follow the standard grammatical rules. Each has to be learned as it does not follow any pattern. For example, *catch* becomes *caught* in the past tense, not *catched.*

Metaphor – A metaphor is a figure of speech in which one thing is actually said to be the other. Example: *This man is a lion in battle.*

Non-restrictive clause – A non-restrictive clause provides additional information about a noun. They can be taken away from the sentence and it will still make sense. They are separated from the rest of the sentence by commas (or brackets). Example: *The principal, who liked order, was shocked and angry.*

Onomatopoeia – Words that imitate sounds, sensations or textures. Example: *bang, crash, prickly, squishy.*

Paragraph – A group of sentences (minimum of two, except in modern fiction) linked by a single idea or subject. Each paragraph should contain a topic sentence. Paragraphs should be planned, linked and organised to lead up to a conclusion in most forms of writing.

Parenthetical phrase – A parenthetical phrase is a phrase that has been added into a sentence which is already complete, to provide additional information. It is usually separated from other clauses using a pair of commas or a pair of brackets (parentheses). Examples: *The leading goal scorer at the 2014 World Cup – James Rodiguez, playing for Columbia – scored five goals. The leading actor in the film, Hollywood great Gene Kelly, is captivating.*

Passive voice – See active voice.

Person (first, second or third) – The first person is used to talk about oneself – *I/ we*. The second person is used to address the person who is listening or reading – *you*. The third person is used to refer to someone else – *he, she, it, they*.

- *I feel like I've been here for days.* (first person)
- *Look what you get, when you join the club.* (second person)
- *He says it takes real courage.* (third person)

Personification – Personification can work at two levels: it can give an animal the characteristics of a human, and it can give an abstract thing the characteristics of a human or an animal. Example: *I was looking Death in the face.*

Prefix – A prefix is an element placed at the beginning of a word to modify its meaning. Prefixes include: *dis-*, *un-*, *im-*, *in-*, *il-*, *ir-*. Examples: *impossible, inconvenient, irresponsible.*

Preposition – A preposition is a word that indicates place (*on*, *in*), direction (*over*, *beyond*) or time (*during*, *on*) among others.

Pronoun – A pronoun is a word that can replace a noun, often to avoid repetition. Example: *I put the book on the table. It was next to the plant.* 'It' refers back to the book in the first sentence.

- Subject pronouns act as the subject of the sentence: *I, you, he, she, it.*
- Object pronouns act as the object of the sentence: *me, you, him, her, it, us, you, them.*
- Possessive pronouns show that something belongs to someone: *mine, yours, his, hers, its, ours, yours, theirs.*
- Demonstrative pronouns refer to things: *this, that, those, these.*

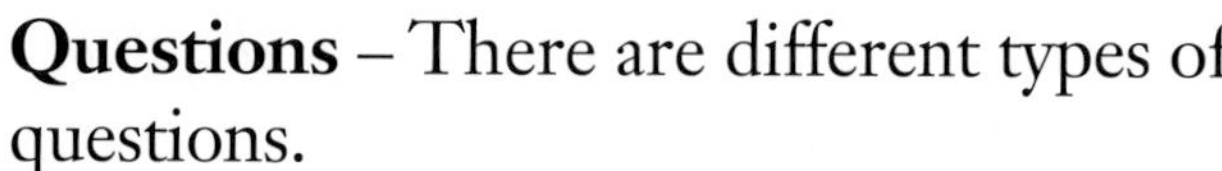

Questions – There are different types of questions.

- Closed questions – This type of question can be answered with a single-word response, with 'yes' or 'no', or by choosing from a list of possible answers. It identifies a piece of specific information.
- Open questions – This type of question cannot be answered with a single-word response, it requires a more thoughtful answer than just 'yes' or 'no'.
- Leading questions – This type of question suggests what answer should be given. Example: *Why are robot servants bad for humans?* This suggests to the responder that robots are bad as the question is "why are they bad?" rather than "do you think they are bad?" Also called loaded questions.
- Rhetorical question – Rhetorical questions are questions that do not require an answer but serve to give the speaker an excuse to explain his/her views. Rhetorical questions should be avoided in formal writing and essays. Example: *Who wouldn't want to go on holiday?*

Register – The appropriate style and tone of language chosen for a specific purpose and/or audience. When speaking to your friends and family you use an informal register whereas you use a more formal tone if talking to someone older, in a position of authority or who you do not know very well. Example: *I'm going to do up the new place.* (informal) *I am planning to decorate my new flat.* (more formal)

Regular verb – A regular verb follows the rules when conjugated (e.g. by adding *–ed* in the past tense, such as *walk* which becomes *walked*).

Relative clause – Relative clauses are a type of subordinate clause. They describe or explain something that has just been mentioned using *who*, *whose*, *which*, *where*, *whom*, *that*, or *when*. Example: *The girl who was standing next to the counter was carrying a small dog.*

Relative pronoun – A relative pronoun does what it says – it takes an idea and relates it to a person or a thing. Be careful to use *who* for people and *which* for things. Example: *I talked to your teacher, who told me about your unfinished homework. This is my favourite photo, which shows you the beach and the palm trees.*

Restrictive clause – Restrictive clauses identify the person or thing that is being referred to and are vital to the meaning of the sentence. They are not separated from the rest of the sentence by a comma. With restrictive clauses, you can often drop the relative pronoun. Example: *The letter [that] I wrote yesterday was lost.*

Semi-colon – A semi-colon is a punctuation mark (;) that separates two main clauses. It is stronger than a comma but not as strong as a full stop. Each clause could form a sentence by itself. Example: *I like cheese; it is delicious.*

Sentence – A sentence is a group of words that expresses a complete thought. All sentences begin with a capital letter and end with a full stop, question mark or exclamation mark.

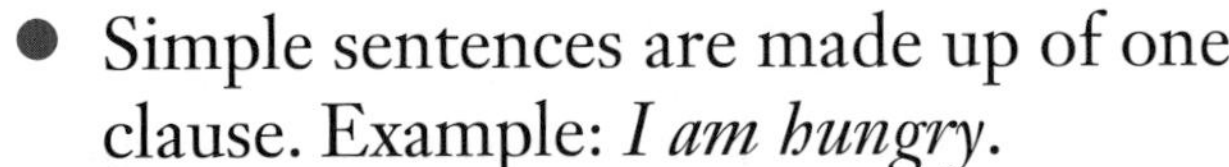

- Simple sentences are made up of one clause. Example: *I am hungry.*
- Complex sentence – Complex sentences are made up of one main clause and one, or more, subordinate clauses. A subordinate clause cannot stand on its own and relies on the main clause. Example: *When I joined the drama club, I did not know that it was going to be so much fun.*
- Compound sentence – Compound sentences are made up of two or more main clauses, usually joined by a conjunction. Example: *I am hungry and I am thirsty.*

Good writers use sentences of different lengths to vary the pace of their writing. Short sentences can make a strong impact while longer sentences can make text flow.

Simile – A simile is a figure of speech in which two things are compared using the linking words *like* or *as*. Example: *In battle, he was as brave as a lion.*

Simple past tense – This tense is used to tell you that something happened in the past. Only one verb is required. Example: *I wore a hat.*

Simple present tense – This tense is used to tell you that something is happening now. Only one verb is required. Example: *I wear a hat.*

Standard English – Standard English is the form of English used in most writing and by educated speakers. It can be spoken with any accent. There are many slight differences between Standard English and local ways of speaking. Example: *We were robbed* is Standard English but in speech some people say *We was robbed.*

Suffix – A suffix is an element placed at the end of a word to modify its meaning. Suffixes include: *-ible*, *-able*, *-ful*, *-less*. Example: *useful, useless, meaningful, meaningless.*

Summary – A summary is a record of the main points of something you have read, seen or heard. Keep to the point and keep it short. Use your own words to make everything clear.

Synonym – A synonym is a word or phrase that means nearly the same as another word or phrase in the same language. Example: *shut* is a synonym of *close*. Synonyms and antonyms can be used to add variation and depth to your writing.

Syntax – The study of how words are organised in a sentence.

Tense – A tense is a verb form that shows whether events happen in the past, present or the future.

- *The Pyramids are on the west bank of the River Nile.* (present tense)
- *They were built as enormous tombs.* (past tense)
- *They will stand for centuries to come.* (future tense)

Most verbs change their spelling by adding *–ed* to form the past tense. Example: *walk/walked.* Some have irregular spellings. Example: *catch/caught.*

Topic sentence – The key sentence of a paragraph that contains the principal idea or subject being discussed.

Acknowledgements

The publisher and authors would like to thank the following for permission to use copyright material:

Franz Kafka: Metamorphosis from The Metamorphosis and Other Stories translated by Joyce Crick (Oxford World Classics, 2009), translation copyright © Joyce Crick 2009, Oxford University Press. Reproduced with permission of the Licensor through PLSclear.

Geraldine McCaughrean: The Kite Rider (OUP, 2007), copyright © Geraldine McCaughrean 2001, Oxford University Press. Reproduced with permission of the Licensor through PLSclear.

Ian Sample: 'Battleship beast: colossal dinosaur skeleton found in southern Patagonia', The Guardian, 4 July 2014, copyright © Guardian News and Media Ltd 2014, reprinted by permission of GNM Ltd.

Noëlla Coursaris Musunka: Adapted article from the website © NOËLLA COURSARIS MUSUNKA, 2017: https://www.noellacoursaris.com/advocacy-philanthropy. Used by permission from Malaika Organisation.

Bill Bryson: Notes from A Big Country: Journey into the American Dream (Doubleday, 1998), copyright © Bill Bryson 1998, reprinted by permission of the Random House Group Ltd; published in the USA as I'm a Stranger Here Myself: Notes on returning to America after twenty years away (Doubleday, 1999), copyright © Bill Bryson 1999, reprinted by permission of Broadway Books, an imprint of the Crown Publishing Group, a division of Penguin Random House LLC. All rights reserved.

Mandy Sinclair: 'A Sunday Morning in Ait Bougmez' from Why Morocco, 26 April 2015, at www.whymorocco.wordpress.com. Reprinted with permission.

Cable News Network (CNN) for extract from 'First man to hike Amazon River ends 2-year, 4000-mile trek', 10 Aug 2010, copyright © CNN 2010. Reprinted with permission.

Katia Moskvitch: Extract from 'Space tourism: how to prepare for a holiday in space', in 'Engineering and Technology' February 15, 2016, published by The Institution of Engineering and Technology. Reprinted by permission.

Denise Levertov: 'To the Snake', copyright © Denise Levertov 1958, from New Selected Poems (Bloodaxe, 2003), reprinted by permission of Bloodaxe Books Ltd; also from Collected Earlier Poems 1940-1960 (New Directions, 1960), copyright © Denise Levertov 1960, reprinted by permission of New Directions Publishing Corp.

Samuel Selvon: Extract from 'A Drink of Water'. Copyright © Samuel Selvon. Reprinted by permission from the Representative Estate Sam Selvon.

Katy Guest: Extract from the article – 'Gender-specific books demean all our children. So the Independent on Sunday will no longer review anything marketed to exclude either sex' written by Katy Guest; 16 March 2014, The Independent. Reprinted by permission.

Tom Lamont: Extract from the article – 'Asteroids: between a rock and a hard place', 20 Sep 2014, copyright © Guardian News and Media Ltd 2014. reprinted by permission of GNM Ltd.

Dylan Jones: 'iPod, Therefore I Am: A Personal Journey Through Music' (Weidenfeld & Nicolson, 2005), copyright © Dylan Jones 2005

Isabel Allende: 'City of the Beasts' (La ciudad de las bestias) translated by Margaret Sayers Peden (Flamingo, 2003), copyright © Isabel Allende 2002, translation copyright © Margaret Sayers Peden 2002.

Responsible Travel for advertisement 'Come and experience a Peru Amazon Rainforest family adventure!' from www.responsibletravel.com.

World Challenge for extracts from their website www.world-challenge.co.uk.

Every effort has been made to contact copyright holders of material reproduced in this book. Any omissions will be rectified in subsequent printings if notice is given to the publisher.